Organizing for Success

Advance Praise for *Organizing for Success* by Ken Zeigler

"Our employees say that *Organizing for Success* has good strategies and tips that are easy to understand and likely to get implemented."
—Jennifer Moriarty, Training Specialist, Hormel Foods Corporation

"Ken Zeigler's material provides practical insights that are easy to grasp."
—Carlyn Houston, Army and Air Force Exchange Service

"Time management is a critical skill that each of us in business, industry, and government must learn. Like other business skills, the learning comes in many shapes and sizes. Ken Zeigler's approach to time management and organization has proven to be both highly effective and easy to comprehend. *Organizing for Success* will be an excellent resource for time-strapped workers, and those of us who train them."
—Jim Pritchert, VACO Education Service Representative, Veterans Administration Learning University

"Ken Zeigler goes right to the heart of the time management and workload challenges facing all of us, presenting the information in a clear, straightforward style. I have benefited considerably by applying these principles in both my professional and personal life."
—Gary Sorg, Senior Consultant, California Commission on Peace Officer Standards and Training

"I found Ken's approach to organization skills to be refreshingly realistic. Ken's approach encourages us to manage our time and resources *within* the reality of our chaotic, over-filled days. Most organization skills books attempt to teach ways to reduce the chaos. Ken encourages us to embrace it."
—Cynthia Lubecke, Manager, Learning and Organizational Development, CCH Tax and Accounting

"In today's business world, where multitasking is the norm, you need an edge. *Organizing for Success* provides real time saving tools in a straightforward and simple manner that not only saves you time, but makes you more efficient. Everyone needs that edge to stay on top and remain focused. Ken Zeigler provides that very important edge. I recommend this book to everyone. It works!"

—Barbara Abelin, Vice President, Human Resources, Cubic Corporation

"Ken Zeigler has provided our employees with the necessary tools to better organize their work, which has resulted in substantial productivity improvement. His methodology is grounded in real life experience and continuous research. *Organizing for Success* is part of our company's core curriculum."

—Paul Schoen, Senior Director of Training and Development, Vertrue, Inc.

"This material has changed my life. I am a self-described 'creative dreamer' with not an organized bone in my body. Which means few of my ideas ever saw the light of day. Ken Zeigler's *Organizing for Success* taught me how to put everything in perspective by breaking down tasks into manageable and logical goals. Now, not only do I dream up brilliant ideas, I get them completed!"

—Elizabeth "Libby" Williams, Senior Human Resources Consultant, Arizona Public Service

Organizing for Success provides a very practical approach to achieving daily tasks. I especially like the concept of 'the veggie principle' that encourages you to handle those 'hard to swallow' tasks early in the day *versus* allowing them to linger and hang over you like a black cloud."

—Morris E. Harris, Field Training Specialist, GCD

"Ken has transformed time management into a new dimension. Our students testify to how useful his material is to their day-to-day job functions. Most claim up to two hours saved per day if these principles are properly applied."

—Rick Orzino, Coordinator, Business and Workforce Training, Motlow State Community College, Lynchburg, TN

"Ken's time management programs are effective in part because he builds on common sense approaches that anyone can use straight from his presentations. He's entertaining and enlightening, well received by line staff and supervisors alike."

—Kathy Lemkuhl Pedersen, PHR,
HR Associate-Benefits/Training, American Red Cross

Organizing for Success

More Than 100 Tips, Tools, Ideas, and Strategies for Organizing and Prioritizing Work

Kenneth Zeigler
President, Zeigler & Sons, Inc.

McGraw-Hill
New York Chicago San Francisco Lisbon
London Madrid Mexico City Milan New Delhi
San Juan Seoul Singapore Sydney Toronto

The McGraw-Hill Companies

3 4 5 6 7 8 9 0 DOC/DOC 0 9 8 7 6

ISBN 0-07-145778-X

This publication is designed to provide accurate and authoritative information in regard to the subject matter covered. It is sold with the understanding that the publisher is not engaged in rendering legal, accounting, or other professional service. If legal advice or other expert assistance is required, the services of a competent professional person should be sought.

—From a declaration of principles jointly adopted by a committee of the American Bar Association and a committee of publishers.

McGraw-Hill books are available at special quantity discounts to use as premiums and sales promotions, or for use in corporate training programs. For more information, please write to the Director of Special Sales, Professional Publishing, McGraw-Hill, Two Penn Plaza, New York, NY 10121-2298. Or contact your local bookstore.

This book is printed on recycled, acid-free paper containing a minimum of 50% recycled, de-inked fiber.

Library of Congress Cataloging-in-Publication Data

Zeigler, Kenneth.
Organizing for success / by Kenneth Zeigler.
p. cm.
ISBN 0-07-145778-X (pbk. : alk. paper)
1. Time management. 2. Executives—Time management. I. Title.

HD69.T54.Z45 2005
658.4'093—dc22 2005002531

This book is dedicated to my best friend and mentor, my father, whose love, understanding, advice, and the way he lives everyday, inspires me to not give up and always strive for excellence.

—KZ

Contents

Acknowledgments

There are so many people to thank who had something to do with this book being published: to Frank Ribaudo at Hertz and the chance he gave me eight years ago; to Ed and Nancy Morris; to all the training officers like Barb Abelin, who have offered suggestions and opportunities to make this book better; to Dean Berry, for giving me my start in training and believing in me; to Jeffrey and Lisa for reading the manuscript, trying out the material, providing ways to improve it, and selling the idea to others at McGraw-Hill; to my mother and father for teaching me that anything was possible and supporting me through the successes and failures; to my biggest fan and main mentor, my father, who my whole life taught me how to lead by example and was always there to listen and offer constructive ideas; and finally to my wife, Mary Beth, and two sons, Zachary and Nicholas, who have never complained about my travel, always been supportive, and never let me forget my mission statement, to actually have a quality personal life and remember what's really important.

Acknowledgments

Organizing for Success

Introduction

How This Book Is Different and What It Can Do for You

Organizing for Success was originally written for the Hertz Corporation in 1996 as a result of analyzing employees' needs for six months. Since then, I have taught more than 25,000 students time management and organizing skills at corporations large and small.

From years of research one thing is certain. The problem is not the tool people use to become organized or keep track of their time. The problem is that each person's skill set is often not strong enough to keep up with his or her workload.

When I look back at my own career, I wish I could tell you I did everything I recommend in this book. I didn't. In fact, I think I succeeded in spite of myself. Have you ever felt that way? I used to get up every morning and immediately start shooting myself in both feet. By the time I got to work, I was already stressed out. But now, I can honestly tell you that I do everything in this book. If I didn't, there wouldn't be any way I could have a personal life and watch my two sons grow up.

THE GOAL OF THIS BOOK

The goal of this book is to provide tips, tools, ideas, and strategies that you can apply to see immediate, measurable improvement, both at work and at home. You will notice that I'm not trying to sell you an expensive day planner or any kind of electronic gadget. There are plenty of those already, and they can be useful tools. Instead, this book can help you use whatever system you currently use more effectively.

This book will have you analyze:

- Why you're doing it
- What you're doing
- When you're doing it

The key to getting organized for success is to determine and analyze when you're working on certain activities and your reasoning for these actions. In other words, use clear thought, step back from the "trenches" of everyday life, and analyze your activities.

THE BEST WAY TO START

I recommend that you keep track of your time for a week before you read this book or take this course. In Appendix A, you will find a Timekeeping Journal expressly for this purpose. I'm constantly amazed that this is one of the few courses to recommend this. Back in 1996, I began recommending the Timekeeping Journal because when I asked Hertz employees what they had done two days before, over 90 percent couldn't specifically recall. Don't you need to know where you're starting from in order to know where you want to go?

So turn to Appendix A right now, if you can. Photocopy the pages you need to begin your own journal. To get the most benefit from these lessons, begin by keeping a journal of how you spend your time for one week. Then, analyze the results. Every principle,

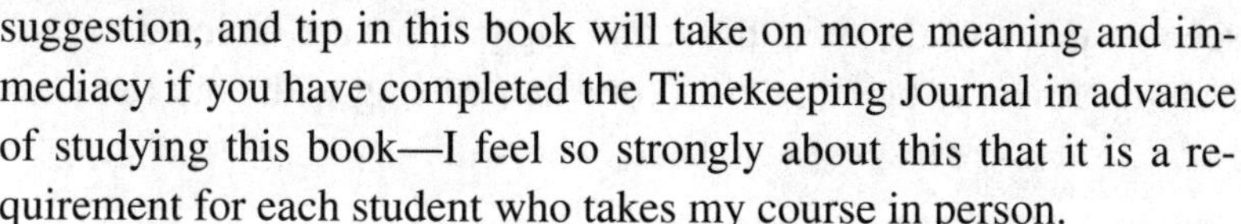

suggestion, and tip in this book will take on more meaning and immediacy if you have completed the Timekeeping Journal in advance of studying this book—I feel so strongly about this that it is a requirement for each student who takes my course in person.

Be sure that you keep track of both your work and personal time. You may wonder, "Why keep track of my personal time?" I believe a personal life is all about quality, not necessarily about quantity. Does what you're doing after work reinforce your personal mission statement? Sometimes a closer look may raise questions and lead to change.

GIVE REALITY A HUG

I'm shocked at how many time management courses talk about the ability to change time and reality. Instead, I say, "Embrace reality and see what you can do to take advantage of it." Rather than acting like a salmon swimming upstream, go with the flow—only add structure and discipline to the flow.

When you keep track of your time for a week, you will see patterns in activities, tasks, interruptions, and unplanned events. Once you see those patterns, use the strategies discussed in this book to handle them more effectively. A major question should be "How do I want to organize my day now that I can see reality?" You'll be amazed at the results!

In addition, you must realize that there are two aspects to saving time and becoming more productive:

1. Improving your time management skills
2. Training others so their time management skills don't kill you

This is another concept that you will probably not see or hear elsewhere. Others try to make you believe that if only your skills were better, everything would be fine. That would be great, but that's not the truth. Time management is also a "team" subject. You will see that many of the tips, ideas, and suggestions are directed toward training others to be more efficient when dealing with you. Remember, if you don't respect your time, who will?

HOW TO USE THIS BOOK

This book is for all people who would like to become more efficient, get more done in less time, and have balance in their life. This book is written as a self-study. All the answers are contained in this book. The answers are often different for each person. Take the ones you like, make positive changes, and discard the rest.

This book is broken down into four key areas to improve your productivity:

1. Keep track of your time, both work and personal, for a week. Your perception of—and the reality of—how long tasks are taking are often two different things. This is your starting point.
2. Make an overall plan, which includes setting goals, to give you a path to get to where you want to go.
3. Make Master, Daily, and Weekly plans—based on reality—that help you achieve your work and personal goals.
4. Use the tips, tools, ideas, and strategies in the last half of the book to manage everything that's bombarding you from all sides, so you can stay focused on achieving your goals.

Use the Time Management Action Plan (Appendix B) in the back of the book to write down the tips, ideas, or strategies that you're going to implement immediately after you finish this book. This activity will strengthen and reinforce your commitment to changing and improving your life, both at work and at home.

LIGHTS, CAMERA, ACTION

The key is action. Pick the ideas and strategies that apply to you, take action, and make them work. Take two or three ideas or strategies at a time and work on them until they become habits. Then move on to two or three more.

It can be easy to get discouraged. For example, I have this conversation all the time a few weeks after a class. The student asks me, "What did you do to me?" To which I respond, "What do you mean?" The student then explains, "Well, after the class I tried what you said and it worked. Then the next day I went back to the old me. Then the new me. Now I don't know who's going to show up tomorrow!" Remember, it can take up to thirty days to reset a habit, so be patient. It will get better if you keep trying.

Any authors or trainers who tell you that their suggestions will work all the time are foolish. But consider this: if this book could make three out of five days better (that's 60 percent), wouldn't you be happy? I am!

1

Taking Control of Your Day: Becoming the Ringmaster Instead of the Beast

The shortest and best way to make your fortune is to let people see clearly that it is in their interests to promote yours.

—JEAN DE LA BRUYE'REFRANCIS BACON

I remember many days of driving to work and feeling like the sacrificial lamb going to slaughter. Not exactly a positive affirmation. Sure enough, right after I got to work the slaughter began. My boss, customers, and coworkers took control of the next ten hours. I used to:

1. Get off to a poor start (courtesy of excessive relationship building)
2. Jump from task to task as a result of a steady stream of interruptions
3. Work on the new interruption or request immediately and drop what I was doing
4. Assume what everyone meant rather than ask questions
5. Spend hours figuring out the meaning of certain e-mail and voice mail messages
6. Write and speak vaguely, which caused more questions to be asked (which in turn took more time to answer)
7. Interrupt everyone else all day and ruin their productivity

I finally realized (after about twenty years) that to become a Ringmaster, I had to:

- Change my thought process. I had more control than I thought, but I had to take the "bull by the horns."
- Be more patient. I needed to slow down instead of running around like a chicken with its head cut off.
- Have more discipline. I had to realize that "there's a time and a place for everything." Successful time managers realize that it's all about discipline. Without discipline, you'll jump from task to task and wonder at the end of the day, "Where did today go?" Following are some examples of how you can become the Ringmaster and take control of your day.

Think of the last circus you went to. Do you feel today more like the ringmaster with a whip and a chair? Or the lion that was being forced to jump through the flaming hoop?

This book is going to give you fourteen lessons on how to better manage your time and get organized for success. You will literally come in contact with more than 100 tips, tools, strategies, and ideas that you can directly apply right away. And some of the ideas will be truly breakthroughs—such as the "veggie principle" (see Chapter 6).

However, none of these lessons will really take hold unless you transform your way of thinking. Consider yourself no longer "the Beast." From now on, you are "the Ringmaster." From this point forward, picture yourself as the master of your time, masterfully controlling the beasts (interruptions, clutter, procrastination, etc.) and looking for every opportunity to take charge, slow down, and impose discipline on your chaotic environment—to take control of your day.

Here are a number of Ringmaster strategies to get the "new you" started.

THE RINGMASTER'S STRATEGIES

1. The number one management skill today is the ability to train others. It would be great if time management were as simple as improving yourself alone. The Ringmaster realized a long time ago that even if he or she had excellent time management skills, his or her coworkers would still make life difficult with their poor time management skills. I had to teach others how to be more specific and brief when writing e-mails and leaving messages for me.

   It is in your best interest to "train" others to ask questions and to ask for help more efficiently. I realized that I couldn't go home on time without a more efficient way to handle the questions and requests I received each day.

   It can take up to thirty days to train others, but isn't it worth it when you realize that it will save you time for the eleven other months in the year?

   I also realized that I was part of the problem. I needed to improve the way I was asking for information and answers from others. I needed to lead by example. I needed to improve the way I left voice mails and e-mails so others would follow my example.

2. When you get into a groove first thing in the morning and a coworker stops by to chat, the Ringmaster suggests talking at break time or at lunch, when it's most appropriate.

   I wanted to be liked. People might start to think I have a bad attitude. How am I going to win Employee of the Month? Then I realized that there is a time and a place for everything.

   I realized that relationship building was all about quality, not quantity. If I set aside time each day to share with and listen to others, the quality of my working relationships would actually improve.

When I started to suggest another time, no one seemed that bothered, especially when I explained that I really wanted to hear their story but because I was so busy I couldn't give it the attention their story deserved.

3. When the Ringmaster gets a request, he or she tries to fit it in where it works best for him or her and still works for the requestor.

   When you drop what you're doing and handle a request the moment it's made, it's 90 percent in their favor and 10 percent in your favor. All you really want is 50/50. Ask if you can *defer* his or her request and "batch" the request with something similar you'll be doing in the near future.

   As an example, I send the bulk of my return e-mails twice a day, once before lunch and once before the end of the day. If the requestor needed something e-mailed, I would ask, "Can I get that to you before lunch or the end of the day?" Then I could batch it with other e-mails.

   Have you ever realized that most people have a greater sense of urgency right before lunch or the end of the day? It helps keep communication brief and to the point.

4. When the Ringmaster gets a voice mail message from someone with little or no information, he or she calls that person back and asks could you please leave your name, your number, the reason for your call, and the best time to call you back when you call in the future. He or she explains that if they do that, he or she will call them back more quickly with the help or information the requestor needs and leave it on their voice mail. This strategy will also cut down on phone tag.

   After that, if the requestor continues to leave poor messages, the Ringmaster doesn't try to figure it out. He or she waits for them to call again. This is called "reinforcing" your request. People are willing to modify their behavior if

they see what's in it for them. Do you really want to play phone tag all day long?

You must *lead by example*. When you leave messages for others, you must be specific by leaving your name, your number, the reason for your call, and the best time for them to call you back. Remember, leave your number twice and don't speak too quickly.

5. When the Ringmaster gets an e-mail that has no subject line and the request is difficult to understand, he or she explains to the requestor how to do it next time so it will take less time for both of them.

   I tell people who send me e-mails to put the reason they're sending me this e-mail in the subject line. Then, in the first three lines of the message, put what they want me to do and when they specifically need it. If it continues to happen after that, I don't respond—I just delete the message.

   The other part of this is that you need to write your e-mail messages in this way for others and be an example. That way, next time they hit the Reply key, they may follow your example.

6. Are you a people pleaser? When the Ringmaster gets a request that is not in his or her area of expertise, he or she directs the requestor to the right person. He or she doesn't try to become an expert on the spot. It is faster for the right person to answer the question or solve the problem than it is for you to try!

7. Improve the way you communicate. The Ringmaster possesses excellent communication skills. One of the fastest ways to improve productivity is to be more specific and detailed with others. This will save time for you and others. This really eliminates questions and misunderstandings.

   When I write and send an e-mail, I try to write it only once and get the correct answer I need immediately. Before I pick up the phone, I make a bulleted list of what I want need or want to talk about. That way, if I get someone's voice mail, I can be brief and to the point.

Being vague may save you time initially when you write the e-mail or leave the voice mail message, but it usually costs you more time in the long run. That's why you need to plan your e-mail message before you begin writing and plan your phone call before you pick up the phone. Planning always saves time.

8. Successful people do one thing at a time. We will examine this further in the section on prioritization. The following is an example.

   The Ringmaster is a "traffic cop" who directs the flow of work that comes across his or her desk everyday. Think of a typical traffic cop. He or she stands in an intersection, motioning for cars in one direction to move forward into the intersection and the others to stay where they are.

   Now imagine what you look like everyday. Is it safe to say that you're motioning in all four directions, allowing all the traffic into the intersection at one time?

   Are you running for cover or getting run over all day long? You could handle your "traffic" more effectively if it was coming from one direction at a time. Tasks will take less time to complete because you'll have more focus and concentration.

An Example

When you're writing an e-mail message and talking on the phone at the same time, do you think the person on the phone can tell you're doing something else? Have you ever put part of your telephone conversation into your e-mail message or part of your e-mail message into your phone conversation?

Either choose the phone call or the e-mail message, and put off the other until you've finished the one you chose. That way both will take less time and you'll make fewer mistakes.

Activity

Using the suggestions discussed in this chapter, write down what actions you're going to take to improve your communication, take control of your day, and save time.

2

The Keys to Successful Goal Setting and Meeting Deadlines

If you don't know where you're going, you'll end up somewhere else.
—YOGI BERRA

The first step in getting control of your time is to know where you want to go and what you want to accomplish. Goals are often set to try to solve problem situations, but some goals are based on the desire for self-improvement.

WHAT IS A GOAL?

A goal is the end result that you direct your time, energy, and resources toward achieving both individually and as a team. It should define the outcome you desire and your purpose. A goal not only can be something to accomplish for your annual review, but also can mean the accomplishment of a project or difficult task.

Whatever the reason for setting goals, you can be sure that the achievement of the goal will result in change. Your goals give meaning to time management. You want to manage time because you want to accomplish certain tasks. A goal is not a to-do item. This is a common mistake. It's something that adds value to the company and/or the individual.

People are always asking for focus and concentration. In this world of distractions, those who can see the big picture and the end result have learned to "sprinkle" the fires around the tasks and projects that "drive" their company.

WHAT A GOAL ISN'T

When I look back at the early goals I wrote, I'm embarrassed. My early bosses never took the time to really explain goal setting, and of course I never really asked. (I'm not sure they really understood its importance either.) Over the years, I have learned the hard way what goal setting isn't. These are some examples of what a goal isn't:

1. It's not a to-do list full of extra work (above and beyond the call of duty).
2. It's not a statement like "I'm going to use more of my sick time this year."
3. It's not a single sentence. It's a sentence that means something followed by a realistic plan for achieving it.
4. It's not something vague like "I'm going to make more money this year" or "Lose weight."

I think my first goal was "I'm going to get a nicer car." (That wasn't too difficult, since I was driving a "bomb" at the time.)

The reason why this lesson is among the first in this book is because organizing is a thought process. Improvement in organizational skills starts with goal setting. It is the foundation. Once you start using the principles in this chapter, the following will happen:

1. Your goals will mean something significant to you, your leader, your division, and your company.

2. You will become part of the locomotive that drives the company.
3. You'll set yourself up to make more money and be promoted more frequently as a result of achieving your goals.
4. You'll meet your deadlines early or, in the worst case, on time.
5. Your daily, weekly, and monthly plans will be focused on improving your performance and the company's.

Now, let's start building that foundation to becoming more organized.

THE PURPOSE OF GOAL SETTING

The purpose of goals is to define a specific end result (desired outcome) and/or solve a problem (or problems), then set a course or path for achieving that end result or solving that problem. Goals provide clear focal points for action. Goals:

- Identify specific opportunities for improved results.
- Establish a clear picture or direction for achieving those results.
- Improve performance by setting accountability for results.
- Provide structure or direction for achieving the results you want.
- Improve communication by promoting mutual agreement on expectations.
- Provide a fair way to reward success.

Companies grow by focusing on ways to make and save more money. In the "heat of battle," if we stay focused on tasks that accomplish those results, we will never be far off track. Companies rarely grow by spending all their time putting out fires.

Benefits of setting and achieving challenging and specific goals for employees include:

- Becoming more efficient
- Being more focused
- Being more productive
- Having more confidence
- Finding it easier to prioritize
- Receiving recognition

HOW TO IDENTIFY OBSTACLES TO ACHIEVING YOUR GOAL

The number one reason why people don't achieve their goals or meet deadlines on time is because they didn't leave room for anything to go wrong. This is a key skill in organization. There is no room for the unexpected or interruptions, in other words, for *reality*.

Obstacles can be tangible or only in one's mind. This is why you should constantly review your progress, check with team members, and try to anticipate changes or potential obstacles *before* they occur. This becomes a two-step process:

1. Identify the obstacle as quickly as possible.
2. Devise a plan to overcome the obstacle and get back on track.

Again, you should have a contingency plan in place *before* you start. Sometimes when we develop a goal, we act like nothing has ever gone wrong in the past. By anticipating potential obstacles, you'll also have less stress when they do come up.

TIP: The past is an excellent indicator of the future. If you carefully examine the past, you will see the typical obstacles that have surfaced in the past and will be able to leave room for them this time.

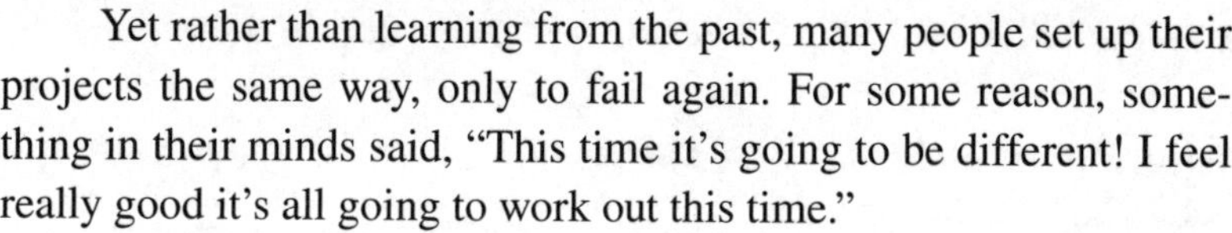

Yet rather than learning from the past, many people set up their projects the same way, only to fail again. For some reason, something in their minds said, "This time it's going to be different! I feel really good it's all going to work out this time."

You may often be given projects and be forced to make assumptions in the beginning. If you make assumptions, be sure that you share them with your boss or whoever gave you the project. Ask as many questions as you can in the beginning to get a good understanding of the desired end result. At the end of each week, review your assumptions and be prepared to make changes.

I see people all the time who start their goal or project based on assumptions, some of which prove correct while others don't. They get to the end of the first week and they don't hit their target for that week, so they say, "See, this goal setting doesn't work!" Don't give up. Add your new information and reset your plan.

When you leave room in your plan for things to go wrong, you have more confidence you're going to meet your deadline. Best of all, when you build time into your plan for things to go wrong and things go pretty well instead, you finish early.

TIP: It is better to underpromise and overdeliver than to overpromise and underdeliver.

Enemy #1: Procrastination

Because goals are often very large with long time frames for accomplishing them, we often procrastinate before starting them. We wait until the pressure and stress build up before we get motivated to start or keep going. Then, many times, we have to reduce the quality of our work just to achieve the goal or deadline on time.

When you are overwhelmed, you're going to have a natural tendency to procrastinate. Accept it, be aware of it, and be willing to work through it.

Enemy #2: Working on Everything but *Your Goal*

Today, we are so focused on putting out the fires that progress toward achieving our goal is very slow or nonexistent.

If your activity doesn't contribute directly toward the achievement of your goal, you may be wasting your time. Without honesty, you may not be able to see you're working on the wrong thing at the wrong time. Remember: putting out fires is a maintenance issue. Putting out fires just helps maintain the status quo. Now, solving the cause of the fire and fixing it: that's something that improves the company and will get you noticed.

Goals are top priorities for most major companies and must receive that placement when you're considering your daily, weekly, monthly, and quarterly plan. Yet many times they look like to-do lists rather than statements that drive a company. You must put your goal-setting plan into your calendar first, because these goals are the highest priority. Otherwise, your daily, weekly, and monthly plans won't be as effective as they could be.

If you follow the previously mentioned steps, you may be able to reduce this problem automatically. That's because effective goal statements are clear, are focused, provide prioritization tools, and provide the structure you need to concentrate on the right activities.

TIP: People are seldom recognized and promoted for putting out fires. People are rewarded for solving the cause of the fire, making the company money, or saving the company money.

As I mentioned earlier, what you want to do is to be sure that you work everyday on tasks that apply to your goals and that you "sprinkle" the fires around them. The trick is that your goals have to go into your plan first, not last, and not at the end of the day. Otherwise, you'll try to put them off until tomorrow, and tomorrow ends up being very close to your deadline!

TO SET ACHIEVABLE GOALS, IT'S IMPORTANT THAT YOU . . .

- Understand how what you do on the job fits into the bigger picture (your team goals, business unit goals, or corporate goals).
- Have a clear vision of what's important to your leader. For example, is your leader working on key initiatives that he or she expects you to contribute to? Remember, your boss gives you your evaluation, determines whether you get a raise or not, and, to a degree, signs your paycheck.
- Ask your internal and external customers for their expectations. Remember: you are the front line. If you ask questions, you might discover information that upper-level management doesn't know.
- Communicate your expectations to others so they will know what they will need to do to help you achieve your goals.

If you aren't focused on these four key practices, chances are that you're working on the wrong things. Successful companies make sure their employees understand how they fit into the big picture. If they don't, how can they be sure everyone is pushing in the same direction?

This brings me to the question, "If you don't know what's important to your boss, how are you prioritizing?" People ask me all the time, "How did you get promoted so much?" I tell them that it's easy: I knew what was important to my boss. (After all, as I said, who does your evaluation and signs your paycheck?)

TIP: If you don't know what your boss's goals are, it's in your best interest to ask!

Finally, in many companies their divisions act independently. To achieve a corporate mission statement, isn't it crucial that each di-

vision identifies what they're going to need from other divisions to achieve their goals? Isn't working together for the good of the company the bottom-line goal?

TIP: Make sure that you check with other groups that you're going to need help from to get their commitment or buy-in before you make a commitment. If you don't, how can you be sure your goal is realistic and achievable?

HOW TO DEVELOP YOUR GOAL

First, brainstorm. If it's a business goal you're working on, the place to start is the list of goals the company has developed. Next, think about what your department needs to accomplish this year as part of the corporate goal or goals. If your goal involves one of the following, you won't be far off. They should involve:

- Safety
- Profitability
- Solving a current corporate problem
- Improving performance

I see so many goals that are simply to-do lists of tasks to be done "above the call of duty." Those are not goals, and they don't drive the company forward. For the value of a company to increase, goals have to increase sales and reduce expenses.

Solving current corporate problems also offers the opportunity to put out fires permanently rather than continue in crisis management. Many people work on these tasks at the end of the day or in the evening. These are the tasks that belong in the morning when you're at your best.

3

Nine Easy Steps to Establishing a Goal

Unless you know where you are going, any road will take you there.
—THEODORE LEVITT

In Chapter 2, we began to learn about setting goals. Here, in Chapter 3, we will walk through the nine easy steps to establishing a goal.

1. SEE THE END RESULT IN YOUR MIND

See it in your mind—close your eyes and picture what your task or project will look like when you reach the end result. Now work backward and write as you go. A major problem is that people tend to leave out obvious steps when they are putting their goal or project together. You will reduce the chance that you'll make this mistake if you really see it in your mind.

By writing down all of the steps needed, including the obvious ones, aren't you educating your boss and others about what's really involved in completing a project or difficult task?

Clearly Define Your Goal in a Statement

The more clearly defined your goal is, the greater the chance you will achieve it. Some examples are:

- To finish XYZ engineering drawing by 11/30 and present it to my boss.
- To completely clean off the top of my desk by 12/31. I must file, throw away, or sign off on each file or piece of paper.
- To receive my master's degree in engineering by the end of the second quarter.
- To increase sales by 15 percent over the same quarter last year.

The biggest mistake I see here is that people try to start at the beginning and work toward the end result.

Write It Down

There is a direct correlation between the amount of writing you do on your project or task and the probability of success. The more you write down, the higher the probability you're going to succeed. The more you write down, the larger the commitment you're making to complete your task or project!

It's like when a computer downloads a picture. When it first appears, it's very fuzzy. As it continues to download, the picture becomes more and more focused until the picture is crystal clear. It's the same concept here.

Begin by brainstorming. See it in your mind, then just start writing about the steps, the tasks, who you're going to need and why, and ideas that come to mind. Just make notes, whatever pops into your head first, in no particular order. Remember: planning and organizing are a task and a checkmark. This will get you going.

Remember, your mind is very visual. When it sees that you've

put a lot down in writing, it sends the message, "We might as well do it; you've already spent all this time writing about it!"

2. IDENTIFY WHEN YOU'RE GOING TO WORK ON IT DAILY AND/OR WEEKLY

Ask yourself, "When, during the course of each day or week, am I going to work on my goal? Why is that time frame the best? Are there fewer interruptions during that time frame? Can I start it first thing in the morning so that I can get it out of the way?"

This is a more important step than you think. By doing this, you'll increase the chance of success. First, you'll be putting the goal into your schedule at a specific time, so you don't put it off to the end of the day; second, you'll be making a commitment; and third, you'll be using clear thought to pick the correct time to work on it.

3. MAKE YOUR GOAL MEASURABLE

By attaching numbers, completion dates, amounts, and so on to your goal(s), you can see if you're making progress or not. You can also use perception, which can be measured by a survey to determine your starting point and whether you're making progress or not.

Measurement is especially important when your goal is spread over a month or longer. At the end of each week, you need to see if you're on target or need to make adjustments to make sure you finish on time.

I see more people give up because they didn't get to where they wanted to be by the end of the first week. Remember, though, in the beginning we're often making assumptions and starting with very limited information.

Cure: stay flexible and anticipate that you're going to have to make adjustments at the end of the first week so you won't get so dis-

couraged. That's why you have to try and build extra time into your plan.

4. IS YOUR GOAL REALISTIC AND ACHIEVABLE?

If you don't believe you can reach your goal, there is a high statistical probability you won't! Have you taken into account situations that could arise that would throw off completing your goal on time? What's gone wrong in the past? Make sure you have a Plan B before you start. When you put extra time into your plan in case things go wrong and everything ends up going right, you'll finish early!

Statistics show that we rarely correctly estimate the time that will be needed to complete a goal or task. Therefore, it's a smart idea to add 20 percent to your estimates to allow for interruptions and unplanned events.

You also need to make sure you have the time and resources to achieve your goal in the allotted time frame. Are you trying to block off too large a time frame to work on your goal daily? If you don't have any spare time now, where are you going to find an extra hour?

Before you decide whether a task is realistic and achievable, check with the people you're going to need to help you and see what their schedules are. Be sure you get a buy-in *before* you start.

Ask yourself:

- Have I done anything like this in the past?
- Who am I going to need?
- What has gone wrong in the past?
- What resources am I going to need?

An Example

In the past, when I had thirty days to work on a project, I would wait until day 29. Then I would be hostile and mobile. I used to

say, "I do my best work under pressure." Oh, really! Do you think I used to cause myself a little stress?

Be sure you have a backup plan, have left room for the interruptions and the unexpected, and have your resources lined up before you begin. Then you'll have the confidence necessary to hit your deadline on time or early.

Believe You Can Do It

In order to complete a project or task on time, it's important that you believe you can do it. Build extra time into your plan to anticipate potential problems. Make sure your plan is realistic and achievable. If you don't believe it's realistic, be sure you say something and explain why!

TIP: No one likes a complainer. If you don't believe the goal is realistic, have a solution before you go to your boss. Become a "solution provider."

5. BREAK LARGE GOALS INTO MANAGEABLE CHUNKS

The number one reason for procrastination is that the project or task seems too large or difficult. How many times have you put off something and had to allocate one whole day to get it done?

By breaking down a goal into 22 workdays a month, you can work on it a little each day and it won't seem so difficult or unpleasant. That way, if you get derailed for one day, it won't be a big deal. You won't feel the same stress because you still have plenty of time to work on it.

Remember to start your goal or project as close as you can to the day you receive it. Don't wait until you're up against the deadline. The day you get the project, start brainstorming. By brainstorming, you're actually moving forward. Just work on it a little everyday instead of having to block out a whole day at the end. You'll have a lot less stress!

As I said, the number one reason why people put off tasks and projects is that they seem too involved and too difficult. Remember, though, that it's better to underpromise and overdeliver than to overpromise and never start.

TIP: The best way to overcome procrastination is to break a task down and work on it a little every day.

Just tell yourself, "I'm only going to work on this for 15–30 minutes. I'm going to see what I'm going to need to do and how I'm going to break the task into smaller parts." (In today's environment, is it very realistic to think you can block off large blocks of time when you usually have a lot of interruptions?)

In the prioritization section, you'll see that we often pick the task that's easiest or that doesn't take a lot of time to complete. When you break that task or project into smaller parts, it will complete with the smaller task you usually pick first. Next time you can't get started, say, "I'm just going to work on this for fifteen minutes."

The more you break down your project, the more writing you'll do. When you finish writing you'll probably say, "Hey, I could probably do this now!"

6. WRITE DOWN START AND COMPLETION DATES

Writing down specific start and completion dates will increase your focus and the likelihood of meeting your goal(s) on time. If you don't do this, chances are you will continue to put off working toward your goal. It's easier to procrastinate until your goal becomes urgent.

If you didn't get a start and/or end date when you got that project, ask for one. If you still can't get one, make one up and tell your boss. Now you have to start.

How many times have you been given a task or project without a deadline, when all of a sudden you get a call and the task or project is now *urgent*? Don't let it happen to you!

Say It

Go ahead, say it out loud. In fact, tell your leader and team members about your project and that you're going to start tomorrow and finish on Friday. Now you have to do it. You're making a commitment. If you have to meet with someone next week to go over your work, schedule the appointment today. Then you'll be planning ahead, anticipating problems, and respecting their time.

7. WRITE DOWN A REWARD FOR FINISHING ON TIME

Start rewarding yourself by simply writing down the history of your successes. As you complete each task you put a checkmark next to it or cross it off. Visual proof of completing tasks makes you feel successful. When you don't write down all the steps, you're not getting all the credit you deserve! The more you write down, the more you will complete, and the more checkmarks you will receive. Don't you want to get the credit you deserve?

Then, when you complete the task or project as a whole, provide yourself an even more tangible reward. It doesn't have to be a big deal. It's part of being good to oneself. The more difficult or unpleasant the task, the bigger you should make the reward. A reward shouldn't always be "a job well done."

Be sure you don't pick a reward that you do all the time anyway. That doesn't really mean anything. Pick a reward that will enhance your personal life. Your reward should be something you can picture in your mind doing, so that when the going gets tough, you can close your eyes and see yourself enjoying your reward. It's like putting the carrot in front of you.

Few of us may want to admit this, but isn't there something inside of us saying, "What's in it for me?" Make your tasks and projects more fun by motivating yourself to complete them.

Create a Reward Before You Start, Not After

Most people don't reward themselves after they complete a difficult task or project. They think that it's just part of their job. They think a reward is a "job well done." Rewarding yourself is part of being good to you.

Some people wait until after they complete a task or project to reward themselves. There's no motivation in that.

A reward doesn't have to be expensive. People say you ought to have a better personal life. Give yourself little rewards along the way. They don't even have to cost anything. Some examples would be:

- If I get this done by noon, I'm going out to eat lunch.
- If I get this done by Friday at noon, I'm going to take a half-day and spend it with the kids.
- If I get this done this week, I'm taking my wife or husband out to that fancy restaurant and a movie.

8. IDENTIFY WHAT COULD GO WRONG

Before you start, be sure you have Plan B. Based on past experience, what has gone wrong? Have you done a similar task in the past? What happened?

The past is a great indicator of the future. Don't quickly dismiss things that have gone wrong in the past. It's like Murphy's Law: if you don't leave room for things to go wrong, things will go wrong. How many times has that happened to you?

What's the worst that could happen if nothing goes wrong? You might finish early? Wouldn't that be a refreshing change?

9. IDENTIFY WHO YOU'RE GOING TO NEED

Be sure you write down in your plan who you're going to need help from and when before you begin.

TIP: Check with them to see if they have the time to help and if your expectations and assumptions are correct before you begin!

Activity

Turn to the goal-setting form located at the back of the book in Appendix C. Using the "goal-setting tips" and "Nine Easy Steps to Establishing a Goal," take a project or task you're currently putting off and write the end result on the line that says "Your goal." It can be work or home related. Make sure you follow all nine steps described on the previous pages.

Make sure you see the end result first and write it down. Then brainstorm and write down the steps needed to complete your task or project as they pop into your head, in no particular order.

After you've emptied all the steps out of your head, then put them into the correct order with deadlines for completing each step.

Is this different from how you're currently organizing your tasks and projects?

4

Organizing, Planning, and Prioritizing: Daily and Weekly

It is more important to know where you are going than to get there quickly. Do not mistake activity for achievement.

—MABEL NEWCOMER

USING A MASTER LIST TO CREATE A PLAN THAT WORKS

This is one of the most important sections in the book. Now that you've learned to set goals and control your day more effectively, it will be important to develop a system to keep track of everything that's bombarding you from all sides. This chapter will show you why it's so important to write more down—then how to organize it more effectively—so you get more accomplished each day.

TIP: The problem is not likely to be the day planner or electronic calendar you're using. Rather, it's probably your skill set. We are going to focus on improving your organizational skills so you can continue to use whatever tool you prefer more effectively. Remember: if organizing takes too long, you'll stop doing it.

Let's start by discussing the most often used "tool" and, unfortunately, the least effective one: the dreaded to-do list. A typical to-do list might contain dozens of items that a person would naively hope to accomplish in a day. It would be hastily scribbled first thing in the morning (after the person arrives late, spills their coffee, etc.), put aside when the first interruption appears, ignored for the bulk of the day, and then, at the end of the day, saved for tomorrow or perhaps thrown in the trash shamefacedly.

The new tools recommended here are not traditional to-do lists. Rather, they are the two key building blocks of staying organized—on a daily, weekly, monthly, and annual basis—the Master List and the Daily List. In brief, a Master List is a pad of paper where you will keep all the possible activities, notes, action items, and so on for an entire week. A Daily List is one piece of paper where you will plan a realistic number of key activities for that day only. (Or the Daily List could very well be kept on your calendar or electronic organizer.) Together, the Master List and the Daily List replace the traditional to-do list. The material that follows explains these lists in detail and how to make the best use of them in combination with your calendar or electronic organizer system.

The Differences between a Master List and the Traditional To-do List

1. The purpose of a Master List is to empty your head of as many thoughts as possible while a to-do list is simply a task list.
2. A Master List is a pad of paper, while a to-do list is a single page or piece of paper.
3. A typical to-do list specifically refers to tomorrow (if you're planning ahead) or today (if you're planning that morning). It puts all the pressure on one day's activities. A Master List is kept for seven days before it starts over.
4. A typical to-do list has to be rewritten each day. The Master List is only rewritten each Friday.

5. A typical to-do list is thrown away after it's rewritten daily. (You're throwing away evidence!) The Master List is saved each week, stapled together, and put in a file; it is used as backup from time to time, and at the end of the year to complete your review.
6. A Master List is larger because it contains not only to-do tasks but also:
   - Meeting notes with action items separated out so you don't forget to do them
   - Notes from conversations
   - Ideas
   - Things you don't want to forget
   - Personal to-do's
   - Tasks with deadlines to add to your calendar
7. With a Master List, everything is in one place. Most people have multiple to-do lists in the form of loose paper or post-its. (Remember, the average person loses forty-five minutes a day just looking for notes and to-dos.)

The Characteristics of a Master List

1. A Master List is updated at the end of each day. At the end of the day, stop responding to e-mails, phone calls, requests from others, and your work. This is your time. With your calendar open and your Master List in front of you, let your mind wander. Brainstorm: write down whatever pops into your head in no particular order. Why do it at the end of everyday? Here are some reasons:
   - Closure.
   - Mental separation between work and home.

- Time and a place for everything. Organizational skills don't take a lot of energy. They're perfect at the end of the day.

Isn't a personal life all about quality, not quantity? How can you have a quality personal life when you're taking work home mentally? We need to turn the lights off mentally when we leave work.

TIP: In productivity, there's a direct correlation between how well your personal life is going and your productivity at work. If you believe this, why don't you treat your personal life with more respect?

2. A Master List is a comprehensive list of everything you have to do and/or don't want to forget. Start by writing all of the tasks that pop into your head. This will be your "grocery list." You want to get an overall view of everything that's waiting to be done.

   One reason for procrastination is that we're overwhelmed. By getting all these tasks and don't-forget-to-do items out of our head, we can think faster, clearer, and even "outside the box."

   The key to organizing is to keep it simple.

> At the end of the day, the concept is that:
>
> 1. An idea pops into your head.
> 2. You write it down.
> 3. Then you delete the thought from your brain.

3. A Master List keeps everything is in one place. So many times we have a list at work, post-its, our personal to-do list on the refrigerator, and notes on the blotter on top of our

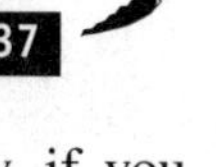

desk. Keep it simple: just have one list. That way, if you look on your pad of paper and can't find it, you probably didn't write it down.

How to Keep a Master List

1. You will be adding to and crossing off tasks on your Master List all day long. Capture new items and tasks on your Master List as soon as you're given them or they pop into your head. This yields big benefits; here's how:

    - A Master List will help you stay focused on the task at hand, because you will not be distracted by trying to remember various other tasks and activities.
    - When you write down tasks on a Master List, now they're in "play" and can be worked into your plan.
    - Keeping a Master List will increase your chances of maintaining your discipline. Write it down and then work on it when you're supposed to, not out of sequence.
    - Chances are that great ideas pop into and out of your head. If you don't write them down as soon as you think about them, you may not think of them again for a while.
    - You can be at home watching TV and think of something worthwhile that you don't want to forget and write it on your Master List so you can enjoy your TV show. If it's a work task, you can deal with it tomorrow, at the right time.

    Don't let a "don't forget to do this" thought take up any space in your brain. Write it down and keep it in front of your eyes. This way, you'll work on it when you're supposed to work on it.

2. Skip lines between entries so you can make notes and it won't get cluttered. Make short notes that can be transferred onto your calendar when you have time or get back to your

desk. If they have specific deadlines, then add them to your calendar where they belong.

In the heat of battle, you need to be able to find notes and to-do items quickly. If you can't, it will cost you time and you'll eventually stop doing it anyway.

Notes are detail. In our overworked society, keeping details is one of the first skills to go, yet it's one of the most valuable skills. Detail will save you time and misunderstandings every time.

TIP: Take notes in your meetings on your Master List so you won't forget what was discussed and everything will be in one place.

I see salespeople who meet with clients and prospects, yet fail to make notes regarding key issues or points that were discussed. Then later, back at the office, they can barely remember what was discussed.

3. Don't try to prioritize or organize Master List entries at first. That comes later. Recording entries on a Master List is supposed to be quick and spontaneous.

   One reason why people don't plan the night before is that when they come into work the next day, with their very detailed and prioritized plan, everything has already changed. You need a plan the night before that's very flexible and can change at a minute's notice; otherwise, you'll go back to flying by the seat of your pants. That's how people become a product of their environment and their day.

   By planning the night before, you'll have about 75 percent of the picture. You won't be able to fill in the rest of the picture until you see the requests waiting for you in e-mail and on your voice mail. Then you can prioritize and get started.

4. Accept the reality that not everything will get crossed off your list. This is going to be a big list, plus you're going to

get more tasks tomorrow. Super Boy couldn't get them all done. Stop putting pressure on yourself!

At the end of the day, this is what helps me go home. I say to myself, if I couldn't get it done today, no one could have. *There is no correlation in productivity between how long you work in a day and how much you accomplish.* It's better to go home, recharge, and prepare to get in early tomorrow, with a full tank of gas, ready to get off to a fast start.

If you stay late night after night, it will become more and more difficult to bring your "A" game first thing in the morning. Your productivity cycles will begin to work against you. After a while, it will take you a triple latte to get started every morning. Respect your recharge time at home at night.

5. Keep your list with you at all times! This will help cut down on "drive-by shootings." A drive-by shooting is when you're walking to the restroom, a meeting, or the break room and someone asks, "Do you have a minute?" Without a list, you'll try to handle the interruption first and it may not have been the right thing to do, or you'll make a promise to do it at a later time and forget about it.

   When you have your list and you get a request, look at your list and see where the request should fit. Don't say yes immediately. You should probably put it on your Master List and come back to it after you finish what you had originally set out to do. This is how you develop discipline.

   Move your requestors away from immediacy! If you handle each request as it happens, your requestors will begin to expect that treatment every time. Is that what you really want? It's an expectation that's hard to live up to every time.

   Unfortunately, we also interrupt ourselves and have a hard time going back to what we were going to do before the interruption occurred.

Review your list throughout the day. When you review your Master List at the end of the day, look for items that need to be scheduled in the future. Add them to your calendar and cross them off your Master List.

Note: If you can't write something down, don't hesitate to leave a message on your voice mail so you don't forget.

6. Keep your Master List all week and then review it each Friday. The game is played for five days, not just one. It's much more realistic than just looking at an individual day to see how you did. This cuts down on transferring to-do items to the next day, which is a waste of time.

   When I came back from taking a Franklin Day Planner course, I had too many tasks written down each day. When I got to the end of the day, I had to move ninety percent of them to the next day.

   After a while, I started to get discouraged. I began to realize that organizing and moving tasks to the next day every night took a lot of time and drained my energy. After six months, I stopped organizing because it took too long. You need to develop an organizational system that doesn't take a lot of time to maintain.

TIP: Remember, if organizing takes too long, you will stop. Rewriting your list once a week really saves time. Also, when you average out all five days, you will actually see you had a pretty good week.

On Friday, see how you did. Only transfer those tasks not completed to the next week. Analyze the tasks you're transferring. Were they veggies or "dessert" items? If a task was a "veggie" and you didn't get it done, what are you going to do differently next week? Staple the old Master List and file it for future use and performance review time.

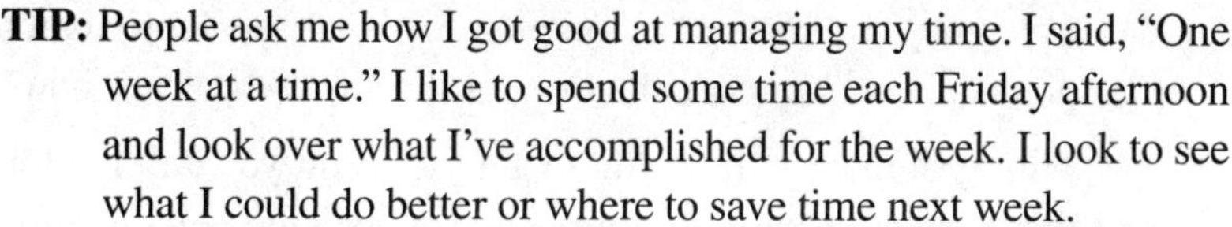
TIP: People ask me how I got good at managing my time. I said, "One week at a time." I like to spend some time each Friday afternoon and look over what I've accomplished for the week. I look to see what I could do better or where to save time next week.

If you really want to improve each week, there's always something you could do a little better at the right time and place.

The Benefits of a Master List

1. Your mind will be able to think faster because it won't be so overwhelmed. Your mind is so bogged down with everything it's trying to remember and keep straight that it really can slow down your reaction time. Getting it down on paper will free up your mind to "think outside the box."
2. You can reprioritize faster and more accurately when new tasks or activities are added. How can you prioritize in the heat of battle when you can't even see all of the tasks on your list?
3. Your Master List will prevent you from shutting down when your day changes or someone throws a monkey wrench into your plan. Don't give up. There's always something to do on your Master List.

   Without this list, your chances of losing focus and procrastinating are greatly increased.

   When someone throws a monkey wrench in my day, my mind used to shut down. I would get frustrated. I would have to take a break and "get my head together, figure out what I was going to do next."

   Now all of my competing tasks are in front of my eyes. My mind seems to say, "No big deal." I can visually just move the order around to fit in the new task with very little lost time and fewer breaks and procrastination.

You may not have accomplished what you originally planned, but you made the most of the day and can see how!

4. This system will allow you to get the credit you deserve for the work you really accomplish. The average person completes somewhere between twenty and forty different tasks in a day, yet many people only have a few tasks written down and checked off by the end of the day.

5. This system will improve your retention. The mind is very visual. The first step in improving retention is writing your tasks down. Next, by keeping your list with you all day, you're constantly reviewing it and improving your retention. By the end of the week, you can see the task and remember what happened without even looking at it.

6. Your list will improve your commitment. The more you write down, the more you'll accomplish. Have you really committed to working on a task if you haven't written it down?

7. A Master List will improve communication. You can show your leader, peers, and/or direct reports what you're working on and what you've accomplished. It will also help you negotiate requests from others. People are more willing to give you more time when they can see the other tasks that you already have on your plate. Your coworkers trust those who write down requests more than those who don't. Make sure they see you writing their request down on your Master List.

   It also helps when you ask your boss, "What are your priorities? What order do you need these tasks done?" Sometimes they will see how much you already have and give the task to someone else.

A Sample Master List

Make handouts for management meeting

Change PowerPoint slides

E-mail available dates to Shirley for Atlanta and Chicago

Call back Shannon 678-456-1212

Call and schedule appointment for car checkup

Call about health insurance

Prepare for 10 A.M. meeting tomorrow

Call ten prospects

Reserve flight to Oakland at the end of June

Balance checking account tonight

Go to Zach's soccer game at 5 P.M. Wed.

Plan weekly staff meeting

Distribute agenda for marketing meeting by Wed.

Learn something new about Outlook this week

E-mail proposal to Member Corp.

Call back Jennifer about operational question by noon

Call Jim about getting together on Thurs.

Purchase flowers for garden at the end of the driveway

Mail thirteen workbooks to Volunteer Tech.

Notes from budget meeting 4/15 (Talked about changing the sales material to add more pictures; asked for more money to increase advertising for more product exposure; Bill agreed to provide new budget figure in one week; set-up next meeting for a week from today.)

ACTION ITEM from meeting, research alternatives for new rollout program by Friday

Call Hector with budget questions today

E-mail product info to Amy

Add Personal Balance to Your List

There are a number of reasons for putting your personal tasks on your Master List.

1. You need to keep your personal life managed and in balance or it will affect your productivity at work. (You'll be thinking about the things you have to get done outside of work but aren't.) Next, your personal tasks start building up. Finally, you get discouraged because you have no personal life.
2. It's easier and simpler to keep everything in one place. Today we have too many lists, they take too much time to manage, and we can't find them anyway.
3. There are certain personal tasks that need to get done during the day, like calling the doctor and going to the bank.
4. There is a direct correlation between how well our personal life is going and productivity at work. If our personal life is so important, why don't we treat it that way by putting our personal tasks on our Master List so they get accomplished?
5. At the end of the day you can see some checkmarks next to your personal tasks so you can see that you have balance and are doing some things to improve your personal life.

TAKE BREAKS BETWEEN TASKS

It's important to keep your mind fresh throughout the day. The mind can only go so long before it "hits the wall." That's why lunch and short breaks are important.

TIP: There is no correlation between how long you sit at your desk and what you accomplish.

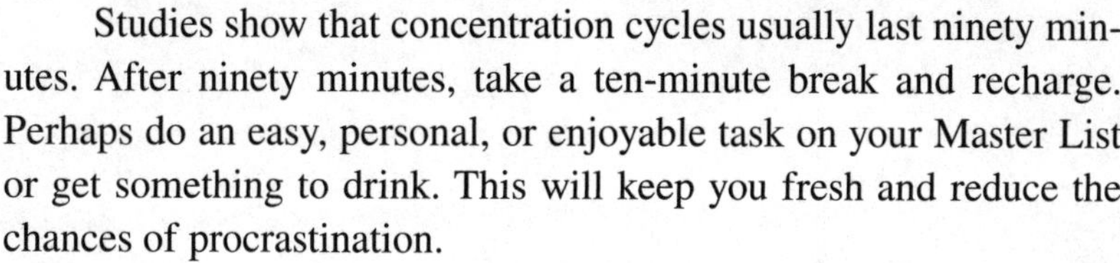

Studies show that concentration cycles usually last ninety minutes. After ninety minutes, take a ten-minute break and recharge. Perhaps do an easy, personal, or enjoyable task on your Master List or get something to drink. This will keep you fresh and reduce the chances of procrastination.

5

Apply the Veggie Principle

In many lines of work, it isn't how much you do that counts, but how much you do well and how often you decide right.
—WILLIAM FEATHER

In Chapter 4, we discussed prioritizing and multitasking quickly and accurately. The fundamental strategy in doing so is applying the "veggie principle." In this chapter, we will continue to build on our strategies for prioritizing and multitasking, but with an emphasis on the veggie principle.

This is the most important principle in the book. A "veggie" is a task, activity, or project that's good for you and your career or personal life but that you have a hard time "eating," or doing first. Without the benefit of training such as this, people will typically start working on a veggie late in the day or when everyone else has gone home. This is ineffective. The true secret to getting the right tasks accomplished at the right time is to apply the veggie principle, that is, tackle first in the day those action items that directly impact your highest goals and priorities. Following the veggie principle is a strategy that will save you time, improve end results, and build your self-confidence.

The veggie principle is a thought process. I use it in everything I do. Here are some examples of how I use it:

1. At work, I start with the most difficult task that has the highest payoff.
2. At home (when I get home at night or on the weekend), I work on the task I like the least so I can enjoy the rest of the night or weekend and don't have it hanging over my head.
3. When I create a meeting agenda, I address the most important issues or topics first so that if I run out of time, everyone can still leave the meeting on time.

TIP: The fastest way to improve productivity is to start each day with a veggie and actually try to get two accomplished before lunch. That way you get off to a fast start, increase your focus, and get more done in the morning *before* lunch. Start using noon as a deadline to get more done.

THE BENEFITS OF USING THE VEGGIE PRINCIPLE IN THE MORNING

- You're more focused.
- You have more energy (because that caffeine just kicked it).
- Studies show that your veggies will take less time in the morning (because for 75 percent or more of the population, the morning is their best energy cycle).
- Your day will flow more smoothly (because you got them out of the way).
- You'll make fewer mistakes (because you're more focused).
- You'll have more confidence and feel great. (What did it feel like the last time you got that task you had been putting off done first thing in the morning? Didn't you feel like you could handle anything after that? You could feel that way every day if you tried.)

Once you are consistently starting everyday with a veggie, see if you can add another one in the morning. Put your two veggies in the morning and try to sprinkle the fires around them. If you don't put your veggies in the morning, they may never get started and/or finished that day!

MAKING AN EFFECTIVE DAILY LIST

To make a Daily List, you can work off your Master List, use a day planner, or use an electronic planner. At the end of the day, after you've updated your Master List, select 2–6 tasks and put them into your paper or electronic plan for tomorrow. How many you put into your plan for tomorrow depends on what you already have scheduled (i.e., meetings, deadlines, and prior commitments). Your list will also depend on how much control you have over your day.

When you come in first thing in the morning, if you start with six, you'll probably find two or three in your e-mail, and two or three important voice mails. Now you're up to 10–12, and that's definitely a full day's work.

TIP: When you open e-mail messages and listen to voice mail first thing in the morning, you're only looking for veggies. Compare those e-mails and voice mails to what you already have on your list from the night before.

Now, place a star next to the two biggest veggies on your list. Typically, the top two will give you 80 percent of the value of all the tasks on your list together. The trick is to honestly identify the two biggest tasks, using the veggie principle. Try to start your day with one of these two, and complete the other before lunch. Don't leave them for the afternoon!

Build your day around your two biggest veggies. Put the two veggies into your schedule first and try to "sprinkle" the fires around

them. Use the other tasks on your Master List as "filler." This will keep you flexible. Try not to move the items on your Daily List to the next day. When you start to make a real effort to get two veggies done before noon, your day will become much easier.

TIP: It's better to underpromise and overdeliver. Say to yourself, "No matter what, I'm going to accomplish two veggies today." Then, try to get ten done. This will help you prevent yourself from going home with a feeling you didn't accomplish anything that day. (Many people plan too many tasks and get nothing done. Has this ever happened to you?)

PLAN THE FOLLOWING WEEK ON FRIDAY

On Friday afternoon, find a quiet place and take out whatever you use to plan your time for next week. Here are some benefits of choosing Friday afternoon:

- You can review the current week while you're still in it and it's still fresh in your mind. You can assess what you accomplished and what needs to move to next week and on what day. You can reflect on:

  a. A job well done

  b. What changes you'll make next week

  c. What you could have done differently

  d. Why a certain task didn't get done

  e. All the checkmarks (which makes it easier to enjoy the weekend!)

- You'll enjoy the weekend more and leave work *at* work! When your plan for next week and Monday specifically is down on paper, you don't have to spend the weekend worrying. You'll gain a sense of confidence that things are "under control."

- Friday afternoon is one of the least productive times of the week. By Friday afternoon, we begin to turn our attention to the weekend. This is an example of a time and a place for everything. Friday afternoon is a perfect time to "reload" for next week. Not only plan next week, but also delete e-mails, throw away paper, file, and clean off your desk. Get ready for the big push on Monday.

I used to end every week on a dead run. When I decided to "front-end" load my week (start working on my most difficult tasks on Monday, not Friday), everything changed. I tried to make the beginning part of the week very difficult and tried to "cruise" into Friday.

Today, I'm basically done with my week by 2–3 P.M. on Friday, so I can use the rest of the day to put closure on this week, figure out how I can handle my work and requests better next week, and put myself in a better position to handle the battle next week.

The game really runs Friday to Friday. On Friday, I'm only going to transfer to next week the tasks I didn't complete this week. I also ask, "If I didn't get this high-priority task done this week, what am I going to do differently next week to complete it?"

HOW TO PUT TOGETHER A POWERFUL MORNING

When I look at the Timekeeping Journals people keep, I focus on the first block of time each day to see what kind of start they're getting off to. The average person spends 1–3 hours checking and responding to:

- E-mail
- Voice mail and the phone
- Checking in with others, checking in with their boss, or "relationship building"

TIP: This time slot needs to be cut down to 15–30 minutes so you can start your first veggie more quickly. This is how to use the veggie principle to your advantage and gain discipline so you get more done *before* lunch.

Here's the new way to start everyday and get more done in the morning:. Let's say you start your day at 8 A.M.

8:00–8:15	When you check e-mail and voice mail first, only look for veggies. Compare the e-mails and phone messages first thing in the morning to the veggies you already have scheduled from the night before. If you see any veggies, complete them, add the others to your list, close e-mail, put the phone on voice mail, and jump into your list. *Turn off your e-mail notification.*
8:15–9:15	Work on your biggest veggie, or important task. This slot is one hour. Try to defer any interruptions that come your way during this hour. Ask coworkers if you could get back to them shortly, as soon as your veggie time is over.
9:15–10:15	Complete your veggie and check e-mail, listen to voice mail, and allow interruptions. Look for the veggies and respond to them as quickly as possible. Allow sixty minutes to complete as many requests as possible.
10:15–11:15	As soon as you're done, close your e-mail, put the phone back on voice mail, and try to defer interruptions for the next short block of time. Go to the second biggest veggie. Try to work on it for sixty minutes.
11:15–11:30	After you finish veggie #2, return lower priority e-mails and phone calls. Get back under control

before you go to lunch. You will notice that people are very quick with you during this time slot. (That's the idea.)

11:30–12:15 P.M. Schedule in a lunch break so you stay fresh for the afternoon. Remember, don't work and eat at the same time. Both will take more time and you won't do either well.

TIP: Take lunch opposite your biggest interrupters. While they're at lunch, it will be quiet and you can get veggie #3 done. When they come back from lunch, you can go. It makes for a shorter afternoon!

12:15 Continue the same idea for the afternoon if possible. You can be less structured in the afternoon if you've been able to follow this plan in the morning. (Direct your interruptions to the afternoon if possible.)

TIP: Most people don't realize this but 90 percent of productivity gains occur in the morning, not the afternoon (unless you're an afternoon person, then the afternoon is the most important).

I used to fly by the seat of my pants. It wasn't until I added structure to my day that I really increased my discipline and what I accomplished.

When you look at the results from your Timekeeping Journal (Appendix A), ask yourself, "What can I do to set up a more structured, disciplined day?" Look for opportunities to schedule veggie time based on the flow of your interruptions.

By setting up time to work on your veggies and batching interruptions and/or fires, you'll be working smarter, not harder.

USE YOUR ENERGY CYCLES TO YOUR ADVANTAGE

Everyone has at least three energy cycles in a day. For 75 percent of us, the strongest cycle is the morning, the next strongest in the afternoon, and the weakest in the evening.

Why does the one in the evening (while you're still at work) often seem the best? Maybe because everyone else has gone home and you don't have any interruptions.

That's why you need to "protect" your "primo" time in the morning. Some suggestions would be to avoid meetings first thing, turn off e-mail, and use voice mail. Try the meetings after you get at least one veggie done or after lunch.

It took me a long time to realize that others were taking advantage of my best time to get things done. They were reducing my most productive time of the day to a "pimple," and I was letting them. When I didn't use the morning to my advantage, it forced key tasks and projects into the afternoon when I was less effective. Because of that, they all took more time to accomplish. As a result, the chances of me having to stay late to finish my work greatly increased. I soon realized that if I could take better advantage of the times in the day when I was most productive, I would have a chance to leave on time.

STOP WORKING LATE AT NIGHT

Stop sneaking over to your computer to check and send e-mail or work on things you didn't get done that day while you are at home. You're only putting pressure on your morning cycle. The later you work, the harder it will be to bring your "A" game first thing in the morning. When you consistently work late at night, you start to build that cushion into your schedule and reduce your sense of urgency to get more done earlier in the day. Remember the saying: there's a time and a place for everything. Say to yourself, "How can I get more done by noon so I don't have to work at home tonight?"

MONDAY MORNING IS CRITICAL

Monday sets the tone for the week. If you get off to a fast start Monday, chances are the rest of the week will be easier and flow better. Make Monday morning your most powerful time by getting the most difficult work out of the way first, then cruise into Friday. A poor start could mean a poor week. If you only get to work early one day a week, make sure it's Monday. Sometimes I get into work at 5:30 A.M. on Mondays just to be sure that a difficult week gets off to a fast start.

TIP: Don't schedule staff meetings or conference calls first thing Monday morning, or any morning for that matter. They just kill everyone's productivity and rob them of their best energy cycle to get more accomplished.

GET TO WORK EARLY AND LEAVE ON TIME

It's better to get to work early and leave on time than to get to work on time and leave late. You should be looking for balance. Most families are much more aware of when you come home late from work than if you leave home early. It's very difficult to have a personal life when you're always coming home late.

An Example

At my house, I want to leave early. No one seems to be in a good mood. But when I come home late, everyone notices. My kids are practically standing by the back door wanting to know why I'm late. The fastest way to get in trouble at home, I learned, is to consistently come home late!

BEFORE YOU LEAVE WORK

The best way to leave work at work (at least mentally) is to organize for tomorrow before you leave work at the end of the day. Many people say they feel out of control when they leave work at the end of the day. There are so many unresolved issues and tasks. Spend the last 10–15 minutes updating your Master List and putting your files away. It's necessary to leave every night with a clean desk. It's very hard to get off to a fast start the next morning when you come in and the top of your desk looks like a tornado hit it. By clearing your mind and desk before you leave work, you'll greatly reduce the chances you'll be thinking about work all night.

DON'T OVERPLAN

Studies show that the average person can only plan 25–50 percent of his or her day. We tend to underestimate, on the average, by 20 percent the time a task will take! Yet day after day, we fill every time slot in our day planners. At the end of each day, it can take up to an hour just moving everything to the next day.

It's as if we're telling ourselves that we're not going to have any interruptions, the phone won't ring with an urgent request, there won't be any meetings scheduled at the last minute, and everything is going to flow smoothly all day long. Accept, instead, that this is going to be a typical day full of interruptions and put it into your plan.

Hopefully, if you used your Timekeeping Journal (Appendix A) properly, you got a big dose of reality. Use that reality to construct a Daily Plan that allows for unexpected tasks, impromptu meetings, and interruptions.

START YOUR MORNING THE NIGHT BEFORE

Think of all tasks that you could do the night before to make the morning easier and more routine. A few ideas:

- Select what you're going to wear tomorrow; iron it ahead of time.
- If you have children, prepare and pack their lunches that night.
- Set the timer on the coffeepot.
- Put the items you're going to take to work by the door.
- Make sure your car has gas.

What could you add to this list? These items cause people to be late and make excuses when they get to work. It also causes their day to get off to a very stressful start. Can you get into a groove before work starts?

BATCH LIKE ITEMS

Do you jump from task to task all day long? Does your day go from phone call, to visit, to e-mail, to interruption, and then start all over again? Does it seem difficult to get anything finished? These are definite symptoms you can correct with batching your tasks and requests. It's very difficult to build any momentum without setting up times to work on activities like e-mail, phone calls, and visits. Look on your list. Are there any similar tasks? Here are some examples:

1. Look on your Master list for phone calls you have to make. Put them together, prioritize them using the veggie principle, and do one after the other for a set period of time. That will give you more focus by creating a sense of urgency. When you're only making phone calls, they'll take less time.

2. Set up periods of time to check and respond to e-mail, then close it.
3. Set up times for visitors and visits to improve their quality and reduce the time needed.

TIP: Set up times each day to specifically respond to e-mail messages, make calls, and see people who need your help. Batching is one of the easiest and most immediate ways to improve productivity.

Activity

Get a pad of paper. At the end of the day, 15 minutes before you leave work write your Master List. As ideas, don't-forgets, or to-do tasks pop into your head, write them down in no particular order. Don't forget your personal items.

Circle any deadlines and identify your 2–6 daily tasks for tomorrow. (They are going to be transferred to your calendar.) Put a star by the two most important tasks. Identify which one you're going to start tomorrow with.

When you're at home tonight, see if you think about work as much.

6

Prioritizing and Multitasking Quickly and Accurately

You seldom get what you go after unless you know in advance what you want. Indecision has often given an advantage to the other fellow because he did his thinking beforehand.

—MAURICE SWITZER

THE BIG THREE

The three biggest reasons why people have trouble prioritizing quickly and accurately are:

1. They try to prioritize without the essential information needed. As you will see, the fastest way to improve how you prioritize is to ask better questions.
2. They let human nature get in the way, so they work on what they'd rather work on instead of what they know (deep down) they should work on.
3. They are given very little information at the time the request is made.

DETERMINING AND HANDLING PRIORITIES

The first step in establishing priorities is keeping track of your time for a week, both at work and at home. Very few people "step back" and look at what they're really doing with their time. Many become products of their environment; they just seem to "go with the flow."

When I took an honest look at my Timekeeping Journal, I realized I was part of the problem and needed to improve the information I was receiving when tasks and projects were given to me. I realized it was faster to ask questions than to guess or assume the right answer. Remember that when you make assumptions, it takes longer and you have a 50 percent chance of being wrong. Why not improve your odds?

(If you have not already completed the Timekeeping Journal in Appendix A, now would be an excellent time to do so. Everyone who does this exercise has unexpected insights from it that motivate them to develop their organizational skills.)

Establishing Priorities

Many people use the "A, B, C prioritizing approach," use some sort of decision-making matrix, or guess. We are going to show you ways to improve the speed and accuracy of your prioritizing.

A, B, C Prioritizing Approach

"A" priorities are *must-do* tasks that have today as a specific deadline to be completed. They should:

- Be important to your leader
- Offer visibility for you and your skills
- Be *vital* to the needs of your customer, peers, or team members

"B" priorities are *should-do* tasks. These are also veggies but don't have today as a specific deadline. As you plan more effectively, these are the tasks you want to work on before they become A priorities.

"C priorities" are *I'd-like-to-do* tasks. These are to be worked on and completed whenever you have extra time.

How to Determine the Correct Priority

1. If you get a vague deadline like "as soon as possible" (ASAP), you must ask, "When do you really need it?" Otherwise, how would you know how to prioritize it against your existing work?
2. You need to know the *reason*, or *why*, a request is so important. Ask questions to determine if the request is really that important.

TIP: Without the specific answers to these two questions, how could you decide the correct urgency and importance of the request? It's difficult to prioritize correctly when you don't have the necessary information.

TIP: When you're making requests to others, you must tell them when you need it and why. You are actually helping others by giving them a deadline and reason so they can accurately prioritize your request. Be sure they understand by saying "yes"; be sure they understand that you're now depending on them to come through.

When you tell someone you need it ASAP, your request will probably go on the bottom of their list. Now they're the Ringmaster (because you've given them control over when they do it) and you're the Beast. Don't water down your deadline because you sympathize

how busy they are. Keep your request and deadline specific as well as why your request is so important. Then you are the Ringmaster.

TIP: When you say "ASAP" instead of giving a deadline and reason, you're giving up control and giving it to them. Put your request in the form of a question to improve cooperation and tone. An example I love is the following:

Could you please turn in your timecards by 5 P.M. this Friday so you can get paid next week?

The Decision-Making Matrix

Time Sensitive Veggie (A)	Not Due Today Veggie (B)
Time Sensitive Master List	Whenever I Can (If I have spare time)

Everything on the left side of the matrix has to be done today, while everything on the right does not. (This is why a specific deadline is so important.)

TIP: To plan more effectively, you should be working on tasks in the upper right-hand box every day so they don't end up in the upper left-hand box. That's how you start to get "ahead of the curve": by working on tasks a little every day, before they're due.

HOW HUMAN NATURE AFFECTS THE WAY WE PRIORITIZE

Oftentimes, we have all the best intentions. We look at our to-do list and select the next activity we're going to work on. Was it or wasn't it the right task? That is the question! When we are brutally honest, we realize that many times we picked the wrong task.

Have you ever reached the end of the day, looked down at your list, and the only tasks left were your veggies? Maybe human nature has more to do with prioritization than you think.

I don't know about you, but human nature can cause me to take a dessert task and make it a veggie. As a great procrastinator, it took me a long time to realize how human nature played a role in how I prioritized. It wasn't until I became honest that my prioritization improved and I began to work on my veggies more often than not.

Do any of these characteristics look familiar?

- We do things we enjoy first.
- We do easy tasks or requests first.
- We do requests or tasks that don't take a lot of time.
- We like to wait until the last minute to start tasks, projects, and goals.
- We like to work on tasks that interest us (because they seem like they take less time).
- We work on the last interruption first and drop what we're currently doing (no matter how important it is).
- We like to work on things we know how to do first and wait on others that need information or training.
- We start small tasks before ones that look large (and difficult).
- We'd rather do others' requests before our own veggie.
- The task selection is often based on habit, not clear thought.

Now that you're aware of the role human nature plays in how you pick your tasks, you need to slow down and consider your motivation for picking certain tasks.

The faster you select and complete the tasks that relate to your goals, your boss, and your key projects, the sooner you can go home everyday.

TIP: People get promoted and receive raises for completing their veggies, not for putting out fires or doing easy tasks that get checkmarks. Think before you pick your next task.

HOW TO NEGOTIATE REQUESTS

When the phone rings, the person on the other end usually tells you he or she needs something done immediately. It's *urgent.* The first question you need to instinctively ask yourself is "Is it really?" This is a tough question.

I used to assume by the tone of a person's voice or his or her position in the company what the priority of the request was. Boy, did I get fooled a lot!

The next time someone calls with a request, ask, "When is the latest I could get that to you?" You may be surprised at the answer. We assume the person needs it now, when perhaps the end of the day or tomorrow would be all right. You're trying to determine where that task falls in your matrix.

Successful people learn how to negotiate for more time so they can finish the important task they're currently working on rather than jumping from task to task.

SUCCESSFUL PEOPLE DO ONE THING AT A TIME

Most people try to do several things at once. Studies show successful people do only one thing at a time. They realize it will take them less time instead of jumping around. They are able to concentrate better, do the job in less time, and make fewer errors.

Consider what it's like when you're talking on the phone and trying to read and write e-mail. Both take longer, and the person on the phone can tell you're doing something else while you're talking to them.

The ability to work on one thing at a time takes *discipline*. Aren't you kind of a traffic cop at work? Successful people either:

- Put off the interruption long enough to finish what they're working on. (This is the fastest way to improve the number of tasks you're completing daily and weekly.)

or

- Accept the interruption because it's a higher priority. When this happens, they make a note regarding important thoughts or ideas, and where they are with the task in the file, then put it back on their list.

SEE IF YOU CAN FIT IT INTO YOUR SCHEDULE

Successful people have learned to negotiate a way to fit the interruption or request into *their* Daily Plan. Can you create a win-win situation where you fit their request into your day when it fits more efficiently for you and still works for them?

This isn't the way I used to think. I used to jump every time I got a request. I realized that I needed to change my thought process. I needed to stop thinking, "Jump first," and instead start thinking, "Where can I fit their requests where it works better for me but still works for the requestor?"

Once I started to ask questions and batch my tasks more effectively, I started to negotiate requests so they fit better into my schedule. But remember, you need to have a Master List, or you will forget these requests and people won't let you work their requests into your schedule.

WRITE DOWN THE TASK AND CIRCLE THE DEADLINE

If you do successfully negotiate a better time to complete the task, be sure that you write down what you've agreed on your Master List. Circle the deadline you've agreed to! Stick to your word. If you don't, you may lose your negotiating privileges with that person in the future!

TIP: If possible, deliver before the negotiated deadline and you'll look like a superstar!

SHOW YOUR LEADER AND TEAM MEMBERS YOUR PLAN

When your leader comes to you with something very important to him or her, show him or her your list. Show your leader what you're working on and what other tasks you have to complete that day. This is impossible to do if you didn't put your plan in writing the night before!

Ask your leader to prioritize your work according to when he or she really needs it by. It's faster and more accurate if he or she determines the priority. See if you can reschedule the other tasks you have, so that you can fit the new one in, or fit the request where it really belongs on your Master or Daily List.

TIP: It's in your best interests to educate your boss as to what you currently have on your plate, existing deadlines, and your abil-

ity to keep track of the huge workload you already have by using your Master List.

Your boss may see that you have a full plate of important tasks already and delegate the task to someone else. The same is true with team members. By showing them your list, they can see what you're working on and what is important to you.

Activity

In the space below, write down ways you could use the strategies discussed in this chapter to more accurately prioritize. Examples would be asking better, more specific questions; avoiding human nature; and working on one thing at a time.

7

Finding More Time in a Day

We shall never have more time. We have, and have always had all the time there is. No object is served in waiting until next week or even until tomorrow. Keep going day in and out. Concentrate on something useful. Having decided to achieve a task, achieve it at all costs.

—ARNOLD BENNETT

THE LAW OF SUBTRACTION

If you're currently leaving work each night at 7 P.M. and you want to be able to leave on time, say 5 P.M., you have to figure out a way to eliminate two hours' worth of activities. You won't find all two hours in one place. It will be more like five minutes here and ten minutes there. When you add it all up, it can be two hours or more. A great place to start is in the morning. You have to examine how you're spending your time each day to find ways to subtract minutes.

The key I've found is to be brutally honest. This was difficult for me to do at first because I was already successful. But the real question should be "Do you want to stay until 7 P.M. every night or do you want to go home and have a personal life?" My mission statement is that I want to watch my two small children grow up. That caused me to make some difficult choices. I had to value my time at work more. I had to look for ways to organize and control myself and my day more effectively; otherwise, I'd never get out of work on

time. This made it easier for me to create a sense of urgency every day.

If, in the back of your mind, you tell yourself you can always fall back on 5 to 7 P.M., how can you create a sense of urgency? The answer is, you can't. Every Friday, when I reviewed what I had done that week, I looked for ways I could improve the following week. Each week, I accomplished a little more in less time. After a year, my life was much different. The key is that you must be willing to embrace change and look for opportunities to save time.

Here are some tools you can use:

- Your Timekeeping Journal (Appendix A)
- Your Master List and Daily List
- Typical fires (interruptions and unplanned events/tasks)

As you look at each activity that shows up in your journal or on your list, ask these two questions:

- Was working on that task or activity the best use of my time?
- Was I doing the right task at the right time?

WHEN YOU REVIEW YOUR JOURNAL

By now, I hope you have completed the Timekeeping Journal exercise in Appendix A. If so, you will find a wealth of insights by reviewing what you recorded. Ask yourself:

- Which activities could be eliminated? (Did they just waste your time?)
- Which activities could I reduce the length of time spent on?
- Which activities could I have delegated?
- Which activities could I have batched with other similar ones?

Take an honest look at each activity you've recorded and identify how you could reduce the amount of time you spend on that type of activity in the future.

How can you use the organizational skills you learned in the previous two chapters to save time by organizing your tasks and projects more effectively? Remember: the morning is usually the time when the fastest improvement can be made.

TIP: The key for most people is to examine the morning. If you're a morning person, that's when you will find the biggest productivity gains. If you aren't a morning person, look at the afternoon.

How could you set up each day more effectively so you could get off to a faster start, have more discipline, and get more done in the morning? Could you move any activities to the afternoon of the previous day?

Activity

Look through the Timekeeping Journal (Appendix A) and answer these questions:

1. Which activities could be eliminated?
2. Which activities could I reduce the length of time spent on?
3. Which activities could I have delegated?
4. Which activities could I have batched with other similar ones?
5. How can I get more accomplished in the morning?

8

Control Your Desk

A place for everything, and everything in its place.

—SAMUEL SMILES

A clear desktop reduces the likelihood of self-interruptions; but when our desks are cluttered, we lose focus. On the average, forty-five minutes are lost everyday hunting for information (paper) on and in our desks. And more and more often, employees are being evaluated on how their workspace looks!

TIP: Think of yourself as a jukebox. A jukebox takes out a CD, plays the selected song or songs, and then puts it back. Then it gets another.

Many people are afraid that a file out-of-sight is a file out-of-mind. But if you want to add focus to your work habits, try to only have one file open on your desk at a time. This way, there aren't any other files on your desk to distract you. The point is, by having one file on your desk at a time, you increase your ability to focus, and your task or project will take less time to complete with fewer mistakes.

Many people use the top of their desk as their to-do list. In fact,

many times their piles actually have names. Remember, though, that you won't take those piles off your desk until two things happen:

1. You can keep the task or tasks you need to complete in each file in front of your eyes by using a Master List or calendar.
2. You can find your files quickly in your file drawer.

An Example

At my son's Montessori school, if you want to play with a different toy, you have to put away the toy you currently have before you can get another one. The point is to only have one file open on your desk at a time so you can increase your focus on what you need to complete. That way it will take less time to complete your task. I bet that's a tough sell!

Here are some easy steps to gain control of your desk.

TAKE EVERYTHING OFF YOUR DESK

Pretend you just moved into your office or cubicle. Take everything off your desk and put it on the floor next to everything else that's already there. Get out the spray cleaner and thoroughly wipe off your desk.

Now, put things back on top of your desk in order of what you use most. To improve my focus and concentration, following is what I did, and didn't, put back on the top of my desk.

Items I Put Back on My Desk:

- The monitor, keyboard, and mouse for my computer
- My phone (If you're right handed, it should go on the right side of your desk. If you're left handed, place it on the left side of your desk.)
- My lamp

- My pen and pencil holder
- My calculator
- A clock
- A plant (dead does not qualify)
- An in-basket
- Blotter

Things I Didn't Put Back on My Desk:

- Personal pictures (they distract you)
- Additional stacking in-baskets
- Candy
- Pen and pencil cup
- Piles of paper and files

In order to gain focus, you must ask yourself, "Is there anything I could do without?" Get rid of all the clutter. Remove old outdated items. Put your pictures out of your immediate sight. People ask me all the time, "Why do I have to move my pictures out of my direct line of vision?" The answer is that when I had pictures on my desk, it was one of the easiest ways to procrastinate. I would look at my pictures and daydream. I would imagine myself in the picture, on the beach, at that wonderful resort. Do you get the picture? You want to eliminate anything distracting so it's just you and your veggie task or project. That way, it will take less time to complete it.

HAVE A CLOCK VISIBLE

Keep the clock in front of you to make you aware of time. It should be a clock that gets your attention. Your perception of time and the reality of how much time you're spending on each activity are often two different things. This is how I use my clock to keep my day moving:

1. When the phone rings, I look at the clock, answer the phone, begin talking, and keep my eye on the clock. It helps me keep the call short and focused.
2. When I check and respond to e-mail, I only do it for a set period of time, then I close my e-mail again and get back to my other work.
3. When people walk into my office, I look at the clock. After a reasonable period of time, I try to sum things up so I can get back to work.
4. I set up specific times to work on my veggies and fires.
5. I use the clock to get the majority of my work done before noon.
6. I use the clock to try to leave work on time.

ORGANIZE YOUR TOOLS

- Empty your desk.
- Go through and cut down on pens, pencils, paper clips, and so on. Do you have enough supplies to open your own Office Depot? Only keep a thirty-day supply.
- Divide your drawers into different areas, for example, stationery, files, and personal.
- Throw away the stuff that mysteriously appeared in your desk.

REMOVE THE FUTURE AND PAST FROM YOUR DESK FILE

The first step is to organize the files that are in the file drawers in your desk. If you want to overcome paper overload, only manage the "present" (what you're currently working on over the next thirty days).

TIP: The "present" is the most important. Treat your desk and desktop like valuable real estate. Only keep what you're currently working on close by. In the file drawers located in your desk, remove the two following types of files and put them on the floor for the time being.

The Past

These are files that have been completed or closed out. The only reason you're going to use them in the future is for reference.

The Future

If you find a file and say to yourself, "Someday I just might need this," or "Someday I'd like to read this," remove it and put it on the floor. At the end, you will put it in your reference file.

HOW TO SET UP YOUR WORKING FILES

Set up your working files in the drawer(s) located in your desk. Organize your files alphabetically or chronologically. These files should typically be at arm's length, either in your desk or very close by. Remember to keep your system simple. Here are some suggestions for setting up a successful working file system.

Suggestions for Setting Up Working Files

- Fingertip info: Phone lists, addresses, and frequently used information
- Current projects: Set up files for each separate project

- Routine tasks: Performed daily, weekly, or monthly
- Clients or prospects
- Problems or issues to be researched

Limit the Number of Categories by Keeping Them Broad

If you have too many categories, you won't be able to quickly find a file anyway. Try to have no more than seven to ten categories.

Create File Names That Make It Easy to Find Your Files

Before you pick a name for a file, think of where you would look for it again in the future if you had to find it quickly. Make your file names interesting.

Don't Put Too Many Papers in Each Folder

Too many papers in a folder will slow you down because you might not find what you're looking for on the first pass. Weed your folders out weekly, and start a new folder if you have to.

Get Honest about What You Really Need

When was the last time you looked at the information you're keeping? Is it outdated? You can only realistically manage so much. If you didn't look at it this week, what are the chances you'll look at it next week? Too much will only slow you down.

TIP: Every Friday, go through your files and see if you have any duplicates or ones you have finished. Throw away extra paper and

put files in the Reference File located across the room so you're ready for next week.

How to Determine Your File Categories

Take out a piece of paper. Look at each of the files on your desk and the ones left in your drawer. Make a note about the topic of each. When you're done, see if there is a way to break them down into seven to ten categories.

Separate the Papers and Folders into Five to Ten Piles

One reason why we put off filing is that our piles are usually large and overwhelming. Make your piles smaller so that you can talk yourself into filing a little each day *at the end of the day*. If you have a lot of files, you may want to make more than ten piles. What's an extra week if you've already put off filing for this long?

At one point in my career, it seemed like I was a year or more behind in my filing. It felt hopeless. Then I broke my piles of paper and files into thirty smaller piles. Every day I worked on just filing a little, at the end of each day. I had everything filed in a month. Since that day when I finished that last pile, I've never gone back to having piles on my desk.

Bring out the Garbage Can and Make It Your Friend

Place it next to you and be prepared to fill it!

Purchase Colored File Folders

Each category in your working files will have a different color. By using different colors, you'll be able to go to the category you want more quickly. *The fastest way to file is to use visual aids like colored file folders*. The eye can pick up the colors much faster.

Get a Box of Manila Folders and a Bold Pen

This way, you'll be able to create a little assembly line. Each time you pick up a piece of paper that needs a new manila folder, reach in the box and grab one. Then take your Sharpie bold marker and write your file name on it. Finally, put the file into the file drawer in your desk, and you're all done.

Handle Paper Only Once

Once you touch a file or piece of paper in one of your stacks, it can't go back where it came from. It must go in one of the five following places:

- The garbage
- The future
- The past
- The present
- Outbound (sign off on it, or delegate it to someone else)

That file or piece of paper can't be placed back on your desk. (Many times, that's why our piles don't get smaller. The paper just goes back into a new pile on our desk.) These five options eliminate questions and the need for new piles.

TIP: When you first look at a piece of paper, make a note on the top what file it should go in. This will save you time re-evaluating it again later! Next time you pick it up, you'll already know where it goes.

STOP USING POST-ITS

If you stop for a second, you'll realize these only add to clutter. It often takes as long to find information written on a post-it as it would have if we hadn't written it down at all. Use your Master List as one central location for all your notes. Note: You may have to slowly wean yourself off the post-its, so be gentle.

PUT THE FUTURE AND THE PAST IN THE REFERENCE FILE

This is the last step because it's the lowest priority. Take the future and the past files and put them in your reference files. This is the tall four-drawer file located in the corner of your office or cubicle. These files contain research for future projects and past projects you have completed. They will typically require three drawers for the past and one for the future.

FILE A LITTLE EVERY DAY SO IT WON'T GET OUT OF HAND

Every time you start a new project, create a file right then. Don't let filing build up.

TIP: Make it a regular habit to file as you go or at the end of each day, and use Friday afternoon to finish for the week.

LEAVE WORK EVERY DAY WITH A CLEAN DESKTOP

Put those files away! Tomorrow is another day. Your Master and Daily Lists should be about the only things left on your desk. Here are the benefits:

- You'll be ready to do battle and get off to a fast start when you come in tomorrow. (It's very difficult to get off to a fast start first thing in the morning when you come into work and your desk looks like a tornado hit it.)
- You'll feel more in control.
- You'll have more focus.
- Your confidential or sensitive files will be kept private.
- If there was a fire and the sprinklers went off, your files would be safe from water damage.

Activity

In the space below, using the suggestions in this chapter, write down actions you could take to keep the top of your desk clean and find files more quickly.

9

Prevent and Limit Interruptions

Be sure, when you think you are being extremely tactful, that you are not in reality running away from something you ought to face.

—FRANK MEDLICOTT

Interruptions come in varying degrees, from worthwhile to simple "relationship building." Interruptions are part of our job, but they can really ruin a day. Here are some reasons why interruptions can be so damaging to productivity:

1. They can slow you down a little or completely derail you.
2. When we have more than one interruption back-to-back, we tend to lose focus.
3. They can make it difficult to stay with one task for an extended period and cause us to naturally hop from task to task.

Let's see what we can do:

WHEN WE ARE INTERRUPTED . . .

- We stop what we are doing.
- We respond to the interruption.
- The interruption ends, and we go back to what we were doing. But, more often, we are off on a new mission.

With your Timekeeping Journal, you have already taken the first major step to minimizing interruptions. You have identified what they are and when and how they occur. In short, you have identified a pattern, the big picture. Now it's time to do something about it!

TIP: Always evaluate your interruptions. Ask yourself, "Is this truly something I must handle right away?"

CRITERIA FOR A WORTHWHILE INTERRUPTION

- Does it relate to one of my goals, priorities, or key projects?
- Is the request important to the needs of a customer, peer, or team member?
- Is it a time-sensitive request from my team leader or boss?

As you can see, not all interruptions are bad. They're a necessity. If an interruption meets the criteria listed above, stop what you're doing and be as helpful as possible. If it doesn't meet the criteria, try to defer the interruption to a better time when you can batch it with other similar requests. Did you notice the similarity between these criteria and the criteria for prioritizing? Let's look at some ways to control interruptions.

I set up times daily to fight fires and handle interruptions. That way, each interruption takes me less time because I'm focused only on it.

Also, realize that there are certain times in a day when interruptions will take less time, like before lunch and the end of the day.

I used to tell my direct reports that if they wanted uninterrupted one-on-one time with me, if they could see me between 11 A.M. and 1 P.M., I wouldn't answer the phone or e-mail. I would just concentrate on what they had to say. That way, I could give what they had to say the proper attention because it was important to me. They really responded well, and it cut down on the "drive-by" visits.

TRY TO CONTROL THE NOISE AROUND YOU

Noise is a tremendous interruption. It's one of the fastest ways to lose focus, making it very difficult to be productive. Do people like to congregate outside your cubicle? Have a team agreement that it's OK to tell each other (without feeling bad) to please keep it down or to use a conference or break room.

Loud voices, speakerphones, and common area noise can really affect your concentration. Have you spoken to common offenders in a polite but firm manner? Have you tried headphones? Protect your veggie time!

TURN YOUR MONITOR

You may not be able to move the desk in your cubicle, but you can usually move your monitor. Move it so you aren't looking directly at the opening of your cubicle. This is an easy way to increase your focus. Sometimes if you look up to see who is walking by, they will take it as a cue to stop and talk to you. Don't give them a reason to stop. (Keep your head down, if you know what I mean.)

CHAIRS IN YOUR OFFICE

If you have chairs in your office, they were probably originally put there to use while conducting business. Now they've become a "target" for colleagues who visit your office. Don't give them the impression "Come on in and make yourself comfortable"! Ask yourself, "How much do I use the chairs for business?"

TIP: Put some files in those chairs (maybe the ones sitting on your desk). Visitors get tired of standing after a short while.

HAVE A "SELECTIVE" OPEN-DOOR POLICY

If possible, keep your door shut during your veggie times, say from 8 to 9 A.M. and from 10 to 11 A.M. Tell people you will be available from 9 to 10 A.M. and after 11 A.M. If they have to come in, it must be your leader or a worthwhile interruption. You'll be sorry if you make exceptions—no one will honor or respect your verbal request! You can keep your door open all afternoon if you want.

I trained my direct reports that if they had to see me during my veggie time, they needed to write down their questions before they got up out of their chair and to be prepared to tell me what they thought the answer was. This was a great way to keep the interruption short and focused. (Most times, my direct reports were actually right, and this strategy built up their confidence.)

TIP: Be sure you discuss this with your leader and gain his or her approval before you institute your new policy.

Reduce "Drive-by Shootings"

MANAGER'S TIP: Try to get out of your office at least three times each morning and go to where your team works before they come to you. See if they have any questions or need anything. That way, you'll be more visible, and you will cut down on the number of "drive-by shootings." You will be the Ringmaster and have more control

over the questions and interruptions that come from direct reports.

PUT A SIGN OUTSIDE YOUR CUBICLE

Put a sign on your door that says:

- Do Not Disturb
- Working on a "veggie" (pin up a picture of broccoli outside your cubicle)
- Today's schedule (so they know where you will be and when your veggie times will be)
- Working on a project (please leave your request on this pad)

WORK SOMEWHERE ELSE

If you can't close your door, try to find a vacant office or meeting room. (Be sure to tell as few people as possible where you are!)

TELL PEOPLE

Often, people don't know how busy you are. Start out first thing in the morning and tell your peers what a tough day you have ahead and that you won't be able to get together with them until after 11:30 A.M. Get to them before they get to you.

Also, spend some time educating the biggest time wasters in your office. Explain your new limited open-door policy. Set times when you'll be free, and get them to agree not to interrupt you until then. You must be firm.

Remember that you must use a friendly, tactful approach so

people don't become defensive. Also, don't always give people free access to your time. Try suggesting a later time when you can block out the interruptions and give them quality time. Remember, it's all about quality time, not the quantity of time you give others.

TIP: Ask your interrupter, "Will this take more than two minutes, because I'm right in the middle of a high priority project?" If it's going to be longer than that, arrange a more convenient time and try to meet at his or her office.

IF YOUR COMPUTER SCHEDULES YOUR TIME

At the end of each day, block out valuable time to get your veggies done tomorrow *before* someone else schedules a meeting in your veggie time! Schedule a meeting in your computer, so you can get your important tasks done!

LEARN HOW TO TACTFULLY INTERRUPT

Successful people know when to interrupt so that the other person doesn't even know what happened. The best way to do this is to wait until they take a breath and try jumping in as tactfully as possible. Practice this first before you try it.

STAND UP

The number one nonverbal way to tell someone that it isn't going to be a long conversation is to stand up when they come into your office or cubicle. Try not to lean against the corner of your desk, since it will make it seem like you have more time. You may have to walk out of your cubicle or office if they don't get the message.

ARRANGE A LATER TIME

Explain to interrupters that you'd really like to talk with them, but you're under a tough deadline. Suggest a better time, like after 11:30 A.M. or during a break or lunchtime. Offer to go to their office or their choice of location. Be careful to make sure they don't think you're too good for them, and don't hurt their feelings. This will increase people's perception that you're all about business and very professional, but still respectful of their feelings.

DON'T PROLONG THE INTERRUPTION

Resist the temptation to add your two cents or a similar story to the interruption. You're only going to make it more difficult to end the interruption swiftly. Carefully pick the interruptions you want to prolong.

AGREE TO A GROUP POWER HOUR

Many groups find after looking at their Timekeeping Journals that they're their own biggest interrupters. Groups are now looking at ways to get more productive *together*. They pick two times in the morning when they agree to keep the noise and interruptions down to a minimum. They call it a "power hour."

They put up signs saying, "Quiet—you're entering the veggie zone!" People may laugh, but it really works!

TIP: Handle interruptions in teams. This way, you may be able to shelter others in your group so they can get more work done, and then switch off so you can get some work done.

DELEGATE THE INTERRUPTION

Often, you're not the appropriate person to answer a question or solve a problem. Resist the temptation to be a "people pleaser," and don't try to solve their problem. Take a quick minute to direct them to the appropriate person. It's faster for the appropriate person to answer their question or solve their problem that it is for you. Be sure you tactfully explain that to them.

Activity

Make a list of your most common or typical face-to-face interruptions. Write down ways that you could use these tools to prevent and limit those interruptions in the future.

10

Manage, Control, and Write More Effective E-mail

If you wish to succeed in managing and controlling others—
learn to manage and control yourself.

—WILLIAM J. H. BOETCKER

E-mail is the most abused form of communication in the workplace today. I believe it's the number one reason why communication in corporate America has never been worse. That's why a number of companies are experimenting with outlawing e-mail once a week. Many think that e-mail is the answer to everything, so the "quality" of our communication has really suffered. It is also one of the easiest ways to waste time under the disguise of doing something worthwhile.

To be effective, you need to really have discipline when it comes to e-mail. E-mail is a love-hate relationship: love to get it, hate what's in it. It's like an emotional roller coaster. I'm drained by the end of the day. In this chapter, we're going to look at:

1. How to control and manage e-mail
2. The advantages and disadvantages of e-mail
3. When to use it versus the phone or a meeting
4. How to write it to get your reader to respond quickly
5. E-mail etiquette

Here are some strategies I use to reduce the time I spend on receiving and sending e-mail.

TURN OFF YOUR E-MAIL NOTIFICATION AND CHECK E-MAIL PERIODICALLY

E-mail is one of the biggest interruptions in today's workplace. If your machine automatically notifies you that you've just received an e-mail, turn that function off, especially in your veggie time. It is better to keep it turned off all day and set up times to check it or, alternatively, to leave it on all day and check it only once per hour.

I have trouble with discipline. If I left my e-mail open all day, I'd respond to it and interrupt myself every time I heard it go "ding." Because of this, I check my e-mail twice in the morning and twice in the afternoon, unless I'm expecting an important message. In that case, I turn on the visual notification to let me know a new message has arrived.

Remember, if your computer goes "ding," human nature is going to tell you to drop everything and answer it right away whether it's a high priority or not. Then your e-mail is the Ringmaster and you are the Beast.

TIP: Tell people that if they have a time-sensitive question or request that needs attention sooner than one hour, they should call you instead.

In the worst case, turn on the visual notification so an envelope appears when a message arrives. That way, you know it's there and can finish what you're working on.

IF YOU HAVE TO CHECK YOUR E-MAIL FIRST THING

First, change your screen view to "Preview" so you can see the subject line and first three to four lines of the message. I don't have time to read the whole message to determine its priority.

TIP: In the first time slot each day, you're only looking for e-mail veggies that have a specific deadline to be done today and their importance is explained.

You need to get your senders to put their purpose in the subject line and what they need you to do and the specific deadline in the first paragraph (discussed in Chapter 1.) Then you can pick a few of the most important messages, respond to them, and close your e-mail.

Use the six tasks you wrote on your Daily List the night before as a filter to determine if an e-mail message is a veggie or not. If a message isn't a higher priority than what you already have on your list, pass on responding to it until the next time you're scheduled to check e-mail. That way, you can get started on a veggie before you look up to discover that it's lunchtime!

Turn on Preview

Auto Preview is available in most e-mail systems (e.g., Outlook and Lotus Notes) and shows you the content of the first three lines of an e-mail message. It will help you determine if the message is one you need to act on immediately or one you can come back to at a later time.

After you're done checking your e-mail, change the view back to normal so your in-box will contract back to one screen.

DON'T USE INSTANT MESSENGER

Most people who I encounter don't have enough discipline to use Instant Messenger. It can instantly ruin your productivity and reduce what you accomplish in a day. I still believe it's more effective to set up a telephone appointment or meeting than to go back and forth in Messenger when you need to have a discussion or ask questions.

By leaving Instant Messenger open all day, you will set yourself up to jump from task to task, and the number of tasks or activities you complete in a day will suffer. We've already discussed how damaging interruptions can be: the decision is yours.

USE COLORS TO CODE YOUR E-MAILS IF YOU HAVE OUTLOOK

This feature allows you to code incoming messages from certain senders (e.g., your own boss) in different colors so they stand out in your in-box. That way, when you open your e-mail, you'll be drawn to those e-mails first.

FLAG MESSAGES OR DRAG AND DROP THEM ONTO YOUR CALENDAR

If you can't reply to, forward, or read a message when you receive it, this option will assure it won't get lost and will keep it "in the loop" until you can. This is available in Outlook.

TIP: If you don't have this feature, drag and drop selected messages onto your schedule when you want to work on them. Keep your in-box clean.

DO IT NOW, DELETE IT NOW

Act on and respond to your messages the first time that you read them. Go through and delete first, then act on the most important ones, and finally file the rest so your in-box stays clean.

WHAT TO DO WITH "SPAM"

Spam can come in many different forms. Delete them immediately and don't even open them. If you open them, it will tell the sender they've reached a "live" e-mail address.

JUST SAY NO!

Tell people by phone or e-mail to take you off that mailing or "CC" list if you don't need to be on it. If you don't say something, it will keep coming!

TIP: Tell your direct reports which projects you want to be CC'd on; otherwise, they'll CC you on everything.

DON'T USE YOUR IN-BOX AS YOUR TO-DO LIST

The fastest way to fall behind and get in trouble is to use your in-box as your to-do list. It's the same as having piles on your desk. The rule is to never have more than one screen of e-mail messages in your in-box. The average person wastes thirty minutes a day looking for e-mail messages. Take action and then file it, file and flag it for future action, or drag and drop it on your schedule when you want to work on it.

CREATE RULES TO MOVE AND "BLOCK" CERTAIN E-MAILS

Set up rules to automatically move your incoming messages into the correct file. That will save you time with sorting your messages. Rules can also block unwanted messages. Rules Wizard in Outlook will guide you through the process.

SET UP ELECTRONIC "FOLDERS" AND SUBFOLDERS

The messages you want to keep should go into folders you set up. Here are some examples:

- Take action immediately (often your leader or customer)
- Pending
- Fingertip reference
- Meetings
- Delegate
- Projects (set up a separate folder for each project)

Be careful not to set up too many folders. Otherwise, you'll never be able to find specific messages quickly. It's better to have subfolders under your main folder categories.

TIP: Make sure your file names are consistent with the files in your desk so you don't confuse yourself.

CLEAN OUT YOUR FILES REGULARLY

Use the same principle you used with your desk. Only keep current files and folders in your e-mail system. Archive the past onto a disk or your hard drive. You'll reduce the clutter in your e-mail account,

have more space (which will speed up your computer), and have the past where you can find it when it's needed.

TIP: At the end of every day and on Friday afternoons, file, delete, and/or archive messages to keep your in-box under control. If you didn't read it this week, what makes you think you'll read it next week?

BATCH YOUR RESPONSES TO E-MAIL

When you are doing one thing at a time, it will take less time. By checking your e-mail at regular intervals (say, four times a day), you can concentrate on handling just your e-mail and finish faster.

Give yourself 15–30 minutes to handle as many messages in your in-box as you can, in the correct priority (using the veggie principle), then close it and work on something else.

IF YOU MUST FORWARD A MESSAGE, GIVE INSTRUCTIONS

Put your comments at the top in the subject line or first paragraph. This will save the reader time. "FYI" doesn't really tell the reader anything. A brief comment will take less than thirty seconds and could save each reader hours.

RULES FOR USING E-MAIL RATHER THAN THE PHONE

E-MAIL	**PHONE**
Need only information	Need an immediate response
Provides a written backup	Need to ask questions
Some respond faster to e-mail	Want to hear someone's voice
Multiple people can receive it	Privacy

E-mail often takes less time than telephoning and can be easier than taking notes, especially when you are busy. E-mail is for information; the telephone is for discussion. If you need a discussion, pick up the phone and call them!

TIP: E-mail technically doesn't have any tone. It's whatever a person perceives you meant when they open your e-mail. If you're not sure how a person will interpret your e-mail message, call him or her instead, or call before you hit the "Send" key so they can hear your voice and understand the meaning of your e-mail.

CREATE A SIGNATURE TO HELP YOUR RECIPIENTS

A simple signature at the end of your e-mails allows your recipients to see alternative ways to reach you. Make sure it includes your mailing address and phone number. Signatures should be no longer than six lines.

IF YOU'RE GOING TO BE "OUT OF THE OFFICE"

Use your e-mail like you would your voice mail. If you're going to be out of the office, adjust your sender's expectation of a quick response by setting up the Out of Office feature. This will tell your sender immediately that you're out of the office for a specific period, so they can contact someone else in your place until you return.

SET UP "SPELL-CHECK"

Most e-mail systems have a spell-check feature. You have to set it up manually. Set it up so that it will always check your messages before they leave your computer. This will save you a lot of time proofing

your e-mail. Remember, though, that you still have to check your grammar!

TIP: If you're worried about grammar mistakes, type your message as a Word document, then cut and paste it into an e-mail message. Word can check your grammar, while e-mail messages are only checked for spelling.

USE YOUR CALENDAR TO SHOW YOUR SCHEDULE

Use your online calendar to show the meetings that you have scheduled, the appointments you've made, and the time you're blocking off to get important projects completed on time. That way, others will know when you're available and the best time to schedule a meeting.

SET UP AUTO ARCHIVE

Outlook is automatically set up in the beginning to archive messages over six months old, every fourteen days. Because of the sheer volume of messages the average person receives today, I recommend changing the archiving to at least every three months.

The messages you archive are easy to find on your hard drive, and it frees up space on the company's e-mail system so it's faster for everyone. This suggestion is better than having someone from IS or IT coming to your desk or doing it without your knowledge.

WRITE E-MAIL THAT GETS RESULTS AND SAVES TIME

E-mail Etiquette

Here are a few simple rules to assure that you don't get in trouble and that get you the results you intended:

1. Your e-mail message is a reflection of you.
2. Your e-mail message is a reflection of your company.
3. Write your e-mail like it is a letter or memo. Don't use shortcuts or symbols.
4. Always reread your e-mail before you hit the "Send" key.
5. If the president of your company received your e-mail, what would he or she think?
6. Only mark your e-mail as urgent when it really is urgent.
7. E-mail is admissible in a court of law, so pick up the phone if it's sensitive.
8. Don't write anything you wouldn't say to someone in person.
9. Use simple formats, and stay away from fancy backgrounds.
10. How well you know the reader and/or the subject should dictate your level of formality and language.

The fastest way to speed up responses to your e-mail messages is to improve your subject line. Use your subject line to tell the reader what your e-mail is about. Don't use it to announce the topic. Make them curious about your e-mail. Make your subject line stand out in his or her in box. All readers want to know:

- Why did I get this e-mail?
- What do I have to do, if anything?
- When do you need it?

The average reader decides in 5–10 seconds whether to take action on your e-mail, file it, or delete it. To create more urgency, move the deadline into the subject line.

People often respond first to the ones that look easy or won't take a lot of time. A reader's first impression when he or she opens your message is the most important. If it looks complicated and difficult to read and/or understand, he or she will often close it.

WHAT IS THE PURPOSE OF YOUR LETTER OR E-MAIL?

Before you begin typing, you need to define the purpose of your message. Many writers find that their letter or e-mail misses the point because their message fails to identify this first. Because many writers begin with background information, they don't really see the purpose until they finish writing the letter or e-mail. Also, they come up with a subject line that's very general.

Are you trying to persuade, inform, ask/respond to a question, or thank someone? After you decide and write down your purpose, you're ready to consider your audience. What kind of style will they respond to?

HAVE ONE KEY POINT OR ISSUE PER MESSAGE

If you discuss too many points, ideas, or issues in your e-mail, the reader will become confused and not remember any of them. What is the main point you want him or her to remember?

If you have multiple issues, action items, or requests, tell the reader in the first paragraph so he or she will know.

CONSIDER YOUR READER OR AUDIENCE BEFORE YOU WRITE

One of the biggest mistakes that most writers make is that they don't take time to consider the reader *before* they begin writing. The more you know about your audience, the more you can customize your letter or e-mail. See if you can visualize your reader as you get to know your reader:

1. Who is your reader?
2. How much does the reader know about your subject? (This will determine how much information or background you'll have to include.)
3. What do they respond best to? Do they like short, to-the-point messages or messages that start out with some small talk?

YOUR MESSAGE SHOULD HAVE THESE THREE CHARACTERISTICS

It should be:

1. Short
2. To the point
3. Easy to read and understand

OTHER SUGGESTIONS

- Keep your first paragraph short (no more than 2–3 lines).
- Put the action you want the reader to take in the first paragraph.
- Always try to finish your message with a deadline for the

reader and a reason why they need to respond by your deadline.

- Write in a bulleted, not paragraph, format when possible.
- Make your e-mail look easy to read.
- Keep your paragraphs short (no more than 4–6 lines in length).
- Keep your sentences short so they're easy to read and understand. Make sure your sentences are less than seventeen words long.
- Keep the tone of your message positive. Check it before you send it.

Activity

Write down the strategies you could use to manage and control e-mail, and to write more effective e-mail that would save you time in the future.

11

Managing the Phone and Using Voice Mail

From time waste there can be no salvage. It is the easiest of all waste and the hardest to correct because it does not litter the floor.

—HENRY FORD

The telephone is one of the biggest time wasters today. It is a very difficult form of communication to control. The problem is that you stop your work when it rings or when you make an outgoing call, so you have to learn how to manage it. A call you make or take can start out worthwhile, then you lose control of it, it goes on and on, and next thing you know you're behind in what you wanted to accomplish that day. Here's what I do to manage the phone more effectively.

KEEP A PHONE LOG

The first step in getting control of the phone is to keep a running phone log for a week. Write down the time, the person's name, the nature of the call, and the actual time the call took. Look for patterns in the calls you receive. The best time to set aside to work on a veggie is when the number of incoming calls seems lowest. If you could

cut 2–5 minutes off every call you made or received, can you imagine how much time you'd save each day? For many, it could be as much as an hour or more. In evaluating your log, ask yourself these four questions:

1. Which calls were absolutely necessary?
2. Could you delegate any of them in the future?
3. Were any of your calls just wasted time, or were you procrastinating?
4. What could you do in the future to reduce your time on each call?

OUTGOING CALLS

Before You Pick Up the Phone, Plan Your Call

The number one way to save time on the outbound calls you make is to plan your call before you pick up the phone.

TIP: Ask, "Why am I making this call?" before you pick up the phone. Also ask, "What is my objective or objectives?"

Have a bulleted outline or agenda regarding what you want to accomplish and what you want to talk about in a prioritized order (using the veggie principle) before you pick up the phone. Keep any necessary information at your fingertips. People will get the impression that you're well organized and don't want to waste your time or theirs. If they have caller ID and see your number, they may be more willing to take your call.

Picking up the phone to make a call without a plan is like going to the grocery store without a list of what you need to purchase. (You go up and down every aisle, eating along the way because you're hungry, so it takes longer. You spend more than you intended. When

you get home, you realize that you forgot the one item you originally went to the store to get, so you have to go back.) I've had phone calls like that; have you?

Batch Your Calls

Set aside time each day to return calls, especially medium- and low-priority calls. Typically, use from 11:30 A.M. to noon and the end of the day to return calls. This is part of the veggie principle—focus on one thing at a time and you'll be more effective. Your calls will take less time because you're only making phone calls.

TIP: It's easier to keep the call short and focused before lunch and the end of the day because people are in a rush to eat or go home.

Prioritize Your Calls

Call back people according to how the call relates to your priorities. Use the veggie principle to determine who to call back first. That way, if you run out of time you will have returned all of the most important calls. The others can wait until your next phone time.

Keep the Call Focused

Lack of focus is the number two reason why phone calls go on forever. State the reason you're calling them first. Have an idea in your mind before you make the call just how long it should take to cover your main points. Stay on the topic you need to discuss. If the call starts to wander, be the Ringmaster and get it back on track. Here are some effective ways to end your call without offending the other person:

- Tell them someone just walked into your office (like your boss, for example).
- Tell them you have to go to a meeting.
- Tell them there's someone on the other line or you have another call.
- Summarize the call and say, "Does that cover everything?"
- Tell them, "I know you're really busy, so I'm going to let you go." (A personal favorite.)

Check the Clock before You Pick Up the Phone

Find a clock and check the time before you pick up the phone. Set a goal of how much time you have to complete the call. Keep an eye on the clock so the call and time don't get away from you. Create a sense of urgency for yourself to achieve the goal of your call in your allotted time.

Make Telephone Appointments

Telephone appointments are also good when you reach the right person but he or she is too busy to talk right at that minute, or when a person is hard to reach but you really need to talk to that person. Immediately, ask when a better time would be to talk and *write it down*. Make sure the person writes down the appointment also! This will allow the other person to hopefully prepare for your future call, which will keep the call focused and structured will reduce the length of time the call takes.

Other Suggestions

- Anticipate possible questions the person you're calling will ask.
- Try to figure out the best time to reach your contact.
- If you can't reach them by phone, don't be afraid to fax or e-mail them a message. If it's really important and you're stuck, go to their office.
- If someone offers to take a message, ask for voice mail. Your message will be more accurate and detailed.
- If you're calling back with or requesting information and don't need to speak with the other person, try to pick a time when he or she isn't there.
- Make notes on your Master List of what you talk about during the phone call. It might come in handy in the future.

INCOMING CALLS

Find a Way to Screen Your Calls

Successful people use their voice mail or their assistant during veggie time to protect themselves so they can get their veggies accomplished. If you have an assistant, meet first thing in the morning, explain that day's schedule to him or her, and have him or her screen your calls. Your assistant can tell lower priority callers that you're in a meeting or your door is closed, and find out when the best time would be for you to return the call.

If you don't have an assistant, use your voice mail more effectively. Let the call go to voice mail during your veggie time, then check it when you finish your thought or task. That way, you will be the Ringmaster because you'll be deciding the priority of the call.

You can research the answer or information the caller needs,

call him or her back, and leave the answer on the person's voice mail without even having to speak to him or her.

If you answer the phone, the call will become the Ringmaster because you'll drop what you're currently doing and try to handle it right away. If it's more important than what you're currently working on, you will need to stop what you're doing, make a note where you are, and take the call.

Otherwise, you can put the message on your Master List and return the call when you finish your veggie. The use of voice mail is discussed more thoroughly later in this book. Of course, if you're in customer service or must answer every call, be sure that you keep the call focused and as short as possible.

Let People Know the Best Time to Reach You

Everyone has to be available to receive calls sometime. Let the people you talk to the most know when the best time is to reach you (and the worst). Give those callers the names of others in your department who can also help them.

Delegate the Call to the Appropriate Person

Often, there may be someone else who could better handle the call because either it's a higher priority for them than it is for you or they have the needed information. Resist the temptation to be a people pleaser. Give the caller the name and number of the correct person, or offer to forward their call to the right person. Explain that it will take less time if the appropriate person handles their call or request.

Assess the Nature of the Call Quickly

Decide how the call relates to your priorities. Is it worth dropping what you're currently working on, or can you call the person back at a time that fits your schedule and the priority of the call better?

Ask the caller, "What can I do for you?' Encourage the caller to get to the point quickly; don't let the caller start talking about the weather! Keep asking questions until you determine the nature of the call.

TIP: Encourage others to plan their calls before they pick up the phone to call you (another Ringmaster strategy). This will help keep the call focused and reduce the chances that they will ramble.

HOW TO EFFECTIVELY USE VOICE MAIL

Many people never change their own voice mail, even if they aren't in the office that day or week. Here are two options that will increase your professionalism:

1. Leave a voice mail message once a week that tells your caller the date of that specific week and your schedule.
2. Leave a new voice mail daily that announces the date and tells the caller your schedule that day.

The Benefits of Changing Your Voice Mail Message

- It will make you sound more professional.
- It will prompt your caller to leave the information you really need to help him or her.
- It gives the caller the impression that voice mail is important to you and that you check it. (It will reduce the chances

they'll hit "0" and ask the operator to page you or transfer them to another member of your team.)

You can also give the caller some options listed below:

- The name of someone else who they can contact if it's important that they speak to someone immediately.
- Another phone or pager number they can use to reach you immediately.
- They can hit "0" and speak to the operator (to be redirected).
- They can still leave a voice mail message.

TIP: This way, you can respect the caller's time so he or she doesn't wait around for a return call if he or she needs an immediate response.

What to Ask for from Your Caller on Your Voice Mail Greeting

- His or her name
- His or her phone number
- The nature or reason for the phone call
- The best time for you to call him or her back if he or she needs to talk (This will increase the chances that the person will be there when you call so you don't play phone tag.)

How this saves you time:

1. You know the caller's name, so you don't have to guess.
2. You don't have to look up the caller's phone number.
3. You can leave the answer on his or her voice mail without actually talking.
4. You can avoid playing phone tag by getting him or her to tell you when to call back.

When You Leave Voice Mail

Try to leave a detailed voice mail in the same way you're asking them to do for you. This is why I plan my call before I pick up the phone. In today's hectic environment, you should assume that when you call someone, you're going to get his or her voice mail. By having a plan before you call, if you get their voice mail, your message will be shorter and to the point. Leave them all the details we just discussed, plus set a deadline for them to respond. Be sure to speak slowly, especially when leaving your phone number, so they can write it down!

TIP: Leave your phone number twice in the message, once at the beginning and once at the end of the message. That way, they won't have to replay your whole message if they missed your phone number the first time they listened to it.

TIP: Don't leave messages longer than thirty seconds, if possible. Otherwise, they may only respond to part of your message or none at all.

Other Voice Mail Tips

1. If you're calling them back with information they requested and don't need to talk, pick a time when they won't be there. (It'll cut down on the conversation time.)
2. If you're requesting information and don't need to talk, suggest they e-mail you with the information you need.
3. Return all voice mail within twenty-four hours if possible, even if it's after hours and you know they're not there. (Perhaps explain the circumstances why you couldn't call sooner.)

4. If you get a voice mail from a salesperson and you're not interested, call back and leave a voice mail that politely says that you're not interested or you'll call when you are. (This will reduce your voice mail in the future and make you seem more professional.)

Activity

On a separate pad of paper, write down all of the calls you take and the calls you make for a week. Write down the name of the person, the nature of the call, and how long it took. Write down ways you could save time on the calls you make and take, as well as ways to use voice mail more effectively.

12

Delegation That Empowers

Conductors of great symphony orchestras do not play every musical instrument; yet through leadership the ultimate production is an expressive and unified combination of tones.

—THOMAS D. BAILEY

Delegation is the act of passing responsibility for the completion of a task to another person. Delegation seems so easy, and you've been told it's one of the most effective time management tools available; yet why does it rarely work, you wonder? From my discussions with managers at Hertz rental car locations in 1996, it was the number one reason they were burning out. Delegation wasn't working well in many instances, but they couldn't understand why.

Early in my career, I didn't understand the importance of delegation. As a result, I worked longer hours than I needed to and my staff depended heavily on me for everything (because I did all the thinking). It took me a long time to understand that I was only as strong a manager as the weakest person on my team. My father said to me one day, just before he retired, "I don't know why I come to work anymore; everyone knows my job." To me, that sums it all up.

Through research and trial and error, I have developed some foolproof steps that, if carefully followed, make it difficult to fail at delegation. Remember, the number one most desirable skill in managers today is the ability to train others well.

In this chapter, we're going to examine:

1. Why we don't delegate more
2. The benefits of successful delegation
3. What tasks to and not to delegate
4. The ten easy steps to successfully delegating

WHY DON'T WE DELEGATE MORE? (THE OBSTACLES)

- We think we can do it faster and better than someone else can.
- It takes too much time and effort.
- We fear mistakes that we'll have to correct.
- We fear losing control; we don't want to let go.
- We lack faith in others (insecurity).
- It's outside our "comfort" zone.
- There is no one to delegate to.

Obstacles for Subordinates

- Lack of ability to do the selected task
- Lack of desire or interest in the task or project
- Inability to see why the task is so important
- Lack of enough information or specific expectations
- Lack of authority

BENEFITS OF SUCCESSFUL DELEGATION

- It will save you an amazing amount of time by using your subordinates' time more effectively.
- It's one of the highest forms of motivation known because it encourages participation or being a "part of the group or plan."
- It develops your staff into a more productive group.
- It encourages trust and cooperation on your team.
- It increases the level of teamwork for your subordinates.
- It saves your company money by having the right person doing the job.
- It allows you to improve your communication skills.
- It will increase your self-confidence and abilities to manage others.
- It will improve your teaching and coaching skills.

THE TEN STEPS TO DELEGATING SUCCESSFULLY

When delegating, the most important thing to remember is to *put it in writing*. This eliminates misunderstanding, improves communication, helps you track the task you delegated, and improves the chances the task will be done correctly and on time. If you delegate a lot, keep a notebook. Managers are delegating so quickly now that they can barely remember who they gave the task to.

Early in my career, I had a boss that never wrote anything down. He would delegate tasks to me, and I (knowing he didn't write it down) would wait to start on the project until he asked a second time. He would say the second time, "Didn't I ask you to work on the XYZ report?" I would say, "No, but I'd be happy to start it right away." After a while he learned; he started writing down the tasks he was delegating, and my loophole was gone!

This is what you'll need to write down:

- The date you assigned the task
- Who you assigned it to
- A clear description of the task and your expectations
- A review and due date
- Notes from your discussion

1. Identify Tasks You Can Delegate

Write down all of the tasks or projects that you're responsible for or that you work on daily, weekly, and/or monthly. Using the criteria below, which tasks or projects could you delegate to your subordinates?

Remember, not everything you do can be delegated. Also, not that you'll run out and do this, but don't try to delegate everything at once. Develop a plan and timetable for delegating tasks you've identified as ones you can delegate. Discuss these tasks or projects with your subordinates, and check for interest level. Sometimes you may be very surprised at who's interested in doing what!

What to Delegate

- Tasks or projects that will benefit the company or division (tasks that mean something)
- Tasks or projects that will improve your abilities or performance
- Tasks or projects that will benefit subordinates' knowledge and confidence

What *Not* to Delegate

- Poorly defined tasks or projects where there's a high risk of failure
- Tasks or projects that require management involvement or decision-making authority

2. Choose the Right Person for the Job

- One of the easiest ways to determine the right person to work on a task or project is to ask your direct reports if anyone has an interest. This eliminates guessing, and a high percentage of the time he or she really is the right person.
- If you choose the person, tell your designee why you have chosen him or her for the task. (Make sure the person has adequate skills, knowledge, and interest to do the job.) A common question I hear all the time is "How do you delegate so it doesn't seem like you're 'dumping'?" This tip will usually eliminate the feeling of being dumped on.
- Be sensitive to his or her feelings. Show your appreciation, especially when you're "dumping" a task on him or her.
- Adjust your expectations to the person's abilities.
- Ask the person to work on it as well as he or she can. You're available only if he or she gets completely stuck. Learning by one's mistakes can be very effective.
- If the person has a question, make him or her write it down before coming to you. It will make him or her more focused. It will also save you time and improve the person's retention.
- Ask the person to batch his or her questions so you can answer them all at once.
- Try starting with smaller tasks and build up, increasing the person's confidence.

3. *Define the Project, Desired Results, and Expectations*

Be sure to set aside uninterrupted time with the person you delegate to so you can explain the task and make sure he or she knows what's expected. Don't assume that he or she knows how to do something. Don't end the meeting without full agreement that he or she completely understands all aspects of the task. Make the task seem important, or it may get put off.

If you are being delegated to and the desired results are vague, start asking questions until you can get a good feel for what your leader wants. Otherwise, chances are that you'll have to do it over again.

TIP: Give your direct reports an example of how you do the task, report, or project so they can follow the same format.

4. *Establish Starting and Ending Times*

Make sure you are very specific about when you want them to start, when you'll be reviewing their progress, and the deadline for the task or project. Get them to put it on their calendar right away. You will write the task and designee in your logbook, along with a follow-up date on your Master List.

TIP: When delegating tasks, give employees sufficient time to schedule, set goals, and include the new assignment in their daily plan.

5. *Agree on a Review Time and Don't Hover*

If you delegate a task on Monday and it's due on Friday, set up a review time on Wednesday. (The review time should be halfway between the start and end date.) This will give you time to make

adjustments, let them work on it alone, ensure the task is a success, and increase their confidence.

6. Make Sure They Have the Proper Training

The number one reason why delegation often fails is the person delegating doesn't have time to train the designee. Make the time to train! If you take the time, you'll only have to train them once and they'll get it right the first time.

I typically like to pick the afternoon to train because it's less hectic, I've finished what I wanted to that day, and it's easier to avoid interruptions.

TIP: If it's a report, show them how to do it (even if you could have done it in the same amount of time yourself) and give them a copy of it.

7. Give the Necessary Authority

Make sure your designee has the necessary authority to gain access to certain files or to get cooperation from others. Send an e-mail message in advance on behalf of your designee to those whose cooperation will be needed so things will run more smoothly.

8. If Possible, Delegate the Whole Task

This will help designees develop the confidence to do the job on their own. Be supportive. This will increase their experience and sense of accomplishment. They will feel like they're a more important part of the team.

I used to see managers all the time have a direct report do most of the work on a project yet claim all the glory. If a direct report is al-

ready doing most of the work on a project, let him or her complete it and share the limelight.

Note: If the whole task at once is too much for them, start with small pieces and build up from there.

9. Share the Spotlight and Give Feedback that Encourages

Give them the credit, and let them make the presentation. Getting noticed is a great motivator. This shows that you are proud of them and they're part of the team.

Be sure that if it isn't done the way you asked, you provide "constructive" criticism and positive motivation so next time it is done right.

10. Accept that Others Can Do the Project as Well

There are many ways to accomplish a task. Who knows—you may learn a new, more efficient way! It's been known to happen.

Early in my career, this was initially difficult for me to accept. When you're a young "hotshot," it's hard to believe someone else can do a task better than you. As I got older and was "forced" because of lack of time to delegate more tasks, I was constantly embarrassed to find out that my direct reports could do certain tasks as well as or better than I could. When I finally matured, I enjoyed watching my direct reports' successes, and I believe that's when I really became a good manager.

ANOTHER SUGGESTION

Remember: even though you delegate the task or project, you must supervise it throughout its completion. You don't want to "micromanage," but you do want to follow the progress of the project or

task. Even though you've delegated the task or project, you're still the one responsible in the end.

Activity

Make a list of all the tasks you're responsible for completing daily, weekly, and monthly. Which tasks could you delegate, and why?

Next, follow these steps:

1. Write down the task.
2. Identify who you're going to delegate it to, and why.
3. Define the task and your expectations.
4. Give it a start date, a deadline, and a review date halfway between the start and end date.
5. Identify when you're going to train the designee.
6. Identify and give designees the necessary authority they'll need to be successful.
7. How will you give them the proper recognition and/or constructive feedback needed?

If you're delegated to, what could you do differently in the future to assure that the delegated task goes more smoothly with the desired results?

13

Planning an Effective Meeting

Why is it that those who have something to say can't say it, while those who have nothing to say keep saying it?

—ANONYMOUS

It seems like everywhere I go today, people have meetings to have meetings, if you know what I mean. Ninety percent of businesspeople surveyed said half the time they spend in meetings could have been spent doing more productive tasks, and the average employee loses thirty-one hours a month in unproductive meetings. Yet why do so few companies (that are supposedly so efficient) spend time and effort improving the quality of their meetings? Let's look at some easy ways to increase the cost-benefit relationship of your next meeting.

Meetings can be very important because they:

- Generate ideas that improve the company
- Are a big part of every company's culture
- Provide structure for discussing ideas and making decisions
- Improve communication and eliminate misunderstandings
- Can actually save participants' time when done correctly

CHARACTERISTICS OF UNPRODUCTIVE MEETINGS

- They're longer than necessary.
- More are needed to get the desired results.
- No one received an agenda in time to prepare for the meeting.
- There is a high level of frustration or multiple misunderstandings.
- Information is poorly managed, and there is poor follow-up after the meeting.
- There are more meetings, and therefore less time to work on veggies.
- No one is assigned to take minutes or notes.
- The leader loses control of the meeting.

THERE ARE THREE TYPES OF MEETINGS

- Informational
- Decision making or problem solving
- Brainstorming

WHAT IS THE GOAL OR PURPOSE OF YOUR MEETING?

The goal or purpose of the meeting determines:

- When to schedule it
- Who to invite
- How long it should take

Seventy-five percent of respondents said they rarely used the goal of the meeting to determine all three of the above points. Con-

sidering the purpose of your meeting, what really needs to be covered, and who really needs to be there beforehand, will automatically improve the productivity of your next meeting!

DO YOU REALLY NEED TO SCHEDULE THIS MEETING?

Before you schedule your next meeting, ask yourself, "Is this meeting really necessary? Am I just having a meeting because we always have one? Are there enough items or issues to cover to make it worthwhile?" Have you ever considered how much it costs to get everybody together? If you did, maybe you wouldn't have scheduled the meeting in the first place.

I have found that many times, people choose the wrong communication vehicle to achieve their goal. Some examples are:

- They choose Instant Messaging or send e-mails back and forth every few minutes, when they should have scheduled a meeting
- They schedule a meeting or conference call to keep everyone updated (no discussion) when they should have sent an e-mail and CC'd the appropriate people.

TIP: If it's an informational meeting (with very little discussion), chances are that e-mail would be a better choice. Remember: e-mail is for information, and the telephone or face-to-face meetings are for discussion.

TIP: If you see e-mails going back and forth, suggest a meeting or phone call, which would actually save time and improve communication.

ASK, "DO I REALLY HAVE TO BE THERE?"

Many times, we go to meetings and wonder why we were asked to come. In your Timekeeping Journal, look at the meetings you attended and answer these questions:

- If I didn't share at the meeting, did I really have to go?
- Could I have sent someone else instead?
- Could I have e-mailed the information they needed to discuss?
- Did I have to be there the whole duration of the meeting? Could I have come later or left after I shared?

INCLUDE ONLY PEOPLE WHO NEED TO BE THERE

Tell people why you're inviting them so they'll show up on time. How many times have you been asked to attend a meeting but left wondering why you had been invited? Don't let others leave your meeting wondering the same thing!

HAVE AN AGENDA AND DISTRIBUTE IT EARLY

I'm embarrassed to tell you how many meetings I've been to or researched over the last twenty years that had no agenda. A lack of an agenda is a tip-off that the meeting is going to be a "bull session," run long, and have limited benefit. I finally learned this lesson and made this rule: if I didn't get an agenda in time to prepare, I didn't come to the meeting unless the leader was the president or CEO of the company. I didn't have the time to waste in unproductive meetings. Remember: if you don't respect your time, who will?

So be sure to give everyone plenty of time to organize their schedules so they can attend your meeting. Chances are that you'll get a much better turnout. Participants can organize and prepare *before* the meeting, which will keep the meeting short.

TIP: Ask others to give you an agenda so you can be prepared to contribute to their meeting (and see if you really need to be there or can send someone else).

State Clear Objectives

The more detail you give, the more focused the meeting will be and everyone will be on the same page before the meeting starts, not after!

TIP: Write the purpose or objective of your meeting on the white board or flipchart at the front of the room so participants will see it when they walk in and throughout the meeting. Also mention it at the beginning of your meeting.

Limit the Objectives

Short, to-the-point meetings are the most effective. Try to limit your meeting to one hour or less! The average person's attention span is 60–90 minutes, yet the clear majority of meetings are longer than ninety minutes. Have you ever looked around the meeting after sixty minutes and noticed participants disengaging or "checking out"? If your meeting goes over an hour, ask yourself what you could do next time to limit the objectives.

I'm constantly amazed at the length of agendas I see and the amount of time there is the cover the material. The participants would have to speak at 78-rpm speed to cover everything on the agenda. The meeting is guaranteed to finish late. Remember that meeting participants always appreciate meetings that finish early. They'll remember you positively when deciding whether to come the next time you schedule a meeting.

TIP: Next time you make your agenda, eliminate the lowest 20 percent of your agenda, and you might finish on time or early.

Bring Up Items from the Last Meeting First

Discuss the action items from the last meeting first. Good minutes will make people accountable, and follow-up will make people pay attention at the meeting. Don't spend too much time on this because everyone should already be prepared. Taking too long to cover the action items from the previous meeting is one of the easiest ways to lose control of a meeting. Keep the meeting moving, so you can get to the veggies.

Organize Your Agenda and Meeting This Way

- One-sixth of the meeting should cover your introduction and minutes from the last meeting (ten minutes of a sixty-minute meeting).
- Four-sixths of the meeting should cover the items on your agenda (forty minutes of a sixty-minute meeting).
- One-sixth of the meeting should put closure on the meeting by summing up the meeting, going over action items for the next meeting, and setting up a date and time for the next meeting (ten minutes of a sixty-minute meeting).

Cover the Most Important Issues First

Use the veggie principle to prioritize your agenda. People are freshest at the beginning of a meeting. Cover the most important items on your agenda first. That way, if people are called away or you run out of time, it won't matter as much because the important items on the agenda have already been covered. This will really help you finish the meeting on time.

Many agendas do the opposite. They start out with the easy items (so they can get them out of the way), and the meeting is guaranteed to run long because the most important issues are left to discuss when the meeting is supposed to be over.

Cover Only the Topics on the Agenda

The number one reason why meetings don't finish on time is that the leader of the meeting loses control of the meeting. Be the Ringmaster so that the meeting sticks to the agenda! A meeting that sticks to the agenda will finish faster, and the next time you schedule a meeting, people will be far more likely to attend. It also presents an organized and professional image.

I'm constantly amazed at how many respondents say that many of the meetings they go to have no real Ringmaster. They also explain how frustrating this is to them. If you have to, take turns being the Ringmaster.

TIP: If other issues come up, write them down on a flipchart; and if there's time at the end of the meeting, you can discuss them. Otherwise, you can save them for the next meeting or schedule another meeting to discuss them.

Have Starting and Ending Times

Just a hint: don't schedule your meeting to begin on an even hour, like 2 P.M. People may perceive your meeting as starting around 2 P.M. When you say 2:10 P.M., however, people will know that you mean 2:10 P.M.! Worst case: if they thought your meeting started at 2 P.M. and they show up at 2:10 P.M., they'll still be on time!

TIP: Close the door and begin at the specified time. Let latecomers know it's not OK to be late.

Establish "fines" for latecomers. Harassment is a powerful motivator. Respect your time and the time of those who came at the scheduled meeting time.

When people come late to a class that I teach, I make an example of the student and ask him or her to sit in the front of the room. (How could you be late for a time management class anyway?) I do it in the form of humor, and the person gets the point. Believe me, word gets around.

Set the tone for the meeting in the first five minutes. By setting an ending time, people can better schedule their day and fit your meeting in. Try to finish your meeting early so that you don't have to use all your allotted meeting time.

Give Assignments to Participants

Make it a team event by giving assignments so that everyone is a part of the meeting. That will get everyone involved and keep them alert.

Possible roles for participants:

- Leader (the Ringmaster): this person is a facilitator and makes sure the meeting sticks to the agenda.
- Note taker.
- Timer: this person makes sure the meeting keeps to specific time limits.
- Tone observer: he or she looks for anger or frustration.
- Door person: this person shuts the door when the meeting begins, sits near the door during the meeting, and advises latecomers what's already been discussed.
- Meeting survey taker: he or she fills out the meeting survey and critiques how well the meeting met its objectives.

Get people involved in your meeting as quickly as you can by asking them to share something like their name, their position, or what they are responsible for talking about at the meeting. This gets the participants engaged and makes the meeting more interesting for everyone.

Keep Minutes

If you don't keep meeting minutes (which many don't), chances of action items being completed by the next meeting are very poor. Minutes are a key ingredient of a productive meeting and accountability.

Often, minutes are used as a reference and are reviewed before the meeting begins and at the beginning of the next meeting. It's important that everyone agrees with what happened at the meeting. If you are taking notes and minutes for a meeting:

- Make a list of the participants before the meeting (so you can check them off when they arrive at the meeting).
- Be familiar with the items on the agenda.
- Follow the agenda.
- Write down the formal stuff (like time, date, leader, and purpose).
- Don't write down everything, only key points that relate to the agenda.
- Ask questions if there is something discussed you don't understand.
- Write up and distribute the minutes right after the meeting.

Eliminate Same-Day Meetings

The rule should be that no same-day meetings are held unless participants have time to prepare. Same-day meetings usually last longer and accomplish less. Distribute your agenda, then schedule the meeting for the next day.

Plan Your Meetings in the Afternoon

Remember: the purpose of the meeting determines when you should schedule it. When possible, plan your meeting in the afternoon unless the meeting could really be considered a veggie. Here are some reasons why meetings are better in the afternoon:

1. People are more prepared in the afternoon. They can use lunchtime to catch up and prepare for an afternoon meeting.
2. When people are in morning meetings, they're thinking about all the tasks that are piling up and they can't concentrate 100 percent, so the meeting takes longer. By putting the meeting in the afternoon, participants can get their veggies out of the way in the morning, so they'll have less on their mind.
3. After a morning meeting it's very difficult to run back and jump into a veggie. It takes time to get started again. In the afternoon, that veggie is already out of the way so you don't have to run back to work.

TIP: In a worst-case scenario, if you have to schedule meetings in the morning, schedule them in the late morning right before lunch. Don't schedule them first thing in the morning and kill everyone's productivity. By planning it late in the morning, people will get hungry, which will increase their sense of urgency and focus, and the meeting will finish on time.

Try Not to Schedule Meetings on Mondays

Remember that the purpose of the meeting determines when you should schedule it. Staff meetings are best on Fridays. You have your meeting on Friday so you can review the progress of the group and get everyone on the same page so they can get off to a fast start on Monday.

I am amazed at how many senior managers and CEOs schedule conference calls on Monday morning, the best day of the week, and kill the productivity of their group or company. By killing the best day of the week, it puts pressure on employees during the remaining four days of the week.

Don't Schedule Meetings Back-to-Back

Look at each attendee's schedule before you schedule your meeting. If they have a meeting before yours, give them adequate time to get to yours. Remember, back-to-back meetings are real productivity killers!

TIP: Consider this: if yours is the second meeting, how mentally available are they going to be for yours after they've just come from a two-hour meeting?

Have Ground Rules for Your Meetings

Companies should establish ground rules for all of their meetings. These ground rules should be published in a visible location in each meeting room. This will create the appropriate standards and structure for each meeting. Many very effective companies already do this, but it's surprising how many don't.

If that isn't the case at your company, publish ground rules be-

fore your meeting or write them on the white board in the front of the room. Go over the ground rules first so that everyone's clear. (After doing this a certain number of times, you can stop doing this if it becomes too repetitious.)

Some examples of ground rules:

- Turn off cell phones, Blackberries, and so on.
- No bringing other work to the meeting.
- Go for focus, momentum, and achieving your objective.
- No canceling at the last minute (you must send someone in your place).
- Everyone should be prepared to share.
- Everyone's opinion matters.
- Everyone is to be treated with respect.
- Get there early so you can talk with other participants, prepare, or get food and/or beverage before the meeting begins.

OTHER MEETING TIPS

1. Send out a reminder thirty minutes before your meeting is going to begin.
2. Excuse yourself if the meeting is running long so you won't be late for your next commitment.
3. Pad your electronic scheduler with an extra thirty minutes after the meeting is supposed to end so you can get something to eat or drink, go to the bathroom, check in, and/or get to your next meeting on time.
4. Block out time on your computer so people can't invite you to a meeting first thing in the morning or during veggie time.

5. Don't schedule conference calls at the end of the day.
6. Be aware of time zone differences when you schedule conference calls.
7. Make sure everyone shares.
8. Use PowerPoint when possible to generate more interest and retention.
9. Write down the main points or ideas on a flip chart or white board.
10. Be sure you know what's expected of you and why you were invited to the meeting.

Activity

Consider a meeting that you've been to recently or a meeting coming up that you have to plan. Which of the tips listed above, if they were followed, would improve the results of the meeting?

OR

Plan an upcoming meeting and put together an agenda using the steps discussed in this lesson. Identify the following:

1. The purpose of your meeting
2. Who you're going to invite, and why
3. The topics on your agenda and the order in which you're going to discuss them, using the veggie principle
4. How you're going to keep the meeting under control so it moves smoothly

14

How to Recognize and Manage Procrastination

Determine that the thing can and shall be done,
and then we shall find the way.

—ABRAHAM LINCOLN

Procrastination is the habit of delaying activities until another day or time. We all procrastinate to some degree and in some form or another. In fact, when I got my first employee review, under the heading of "Procrastination," it said "Above Average." As someone who used to procrastinate exceptionally well, I'm going to share some strategies I use to keep it in check and under control.

It's important to recognize:

1. When we are procrastinating, and why
2. What our favorite replacement activities are
3. Steps we can take to manage and overcome our procrastination

MAJOR CAUSES OF PROCRASTINATION

- The task is unpleasant.
- The task is difficult.

- I'm overwhelmed (I have too many tasks to pick from).
- I have too many interruptions back-to-back.
- I'm not organized, or I lack information.
- I don't have clear or written goals.
- I'm not in the mood.
- I don't see why this task is so important.
- I don't have time now.
- This isn't due for a while.

Note: When you put two or more of these together, you're guaranteed to put off that important task or project.

Activity

Answer the following questions:

1. What things do you put off most often?
2. What things are you currently putting off?
3. How do you know when you're procrastinating? Do you have a favorite set of replacement activities? What activities do you choose instead of doing the task you know you have to complete?

HOW TO MANAGE PROCRASTINATION

The following suggestions, when properly used, can help you trick yourself out of procrastinating and into action.

Set Goals and Deadlines

As you learned in the goal-setting chapters (Chapters 2 and 3), one of the leading causes of procrastination is lack of written, well-defined goals. When we have clearly written detailed goals with a specific, well-thought-out plan of action, it makes it easier to set priorities and get started. Your mind figures, "If I've put in this much time, I might as well get started." It's all about making the commitment.

TIPS: 1. Make sure your goals are realistic and achievable.

2. Start difficult or unpleasant tasks during your most productive time. You'll finish them more quickly.

Do It Once

Have you ever noticed how many piles of papers are on your desk or how many e-mails are in your in-box? When you first receive a piece of paper, make a note on the top of it where it belongs, or put the task required on your Master List and file it. When you get an e-mail take action on it, file it, or delete it. Don't let your work pile up, and stop duplicating activities when possible. Many times, your Timekeeping Journal will show you the activities you often repeat.

Break Down the Job into Smaller Parts

A human tendency is to start tasks that we perceive take short amounts of time. The number one way to overcome procrastination is to break your larger task into smaller ones that take about 20–30 minutes to complete. In today's busy workplace, it's much easier to find twenty or thirty minutes than it is to find an hour or more. By completing smaller tasks, you'll build confidence to get the job done.

Remember: if the task looks easy and won't take much time, human nature will cause you to choose that task before others.

TIP: This is how I use "underpromise-overdeliver" to work through procrastination. I say to myself, "I'm only going to work on a task or project for fifteen minutes." Next thing I know, no one has interrupted me, so I keep going. Then, I start to get interested and have some success. Finally, I look up at the clock and I've been working on it for two hours. It's better to start small than to never start at all!

Cut Down on Interruptions

Interruptions derail us from getting things done. "I could have gotten it done, but the phone rang every five minutes." We're not talking about worthwhile interruptions. We're talking about limiting *unnecessary* ones. As mentioned earlier, when we are interrupted, it can often take hours, or even days, to come back to what we were working on. When I get interrupted four to five times in a row, I lose focus, and my mind says, "You need a break." That's why I really try to block out time each day to get my veggies done.

TIP: By reducing interruptions, we can concentrate better and finish the task much sooner. Defer the interruption by negotiating a better time for the activity or letting the call go to voice mail, so you can complete the task you're currently working on.

Let Others Know of Your Goal and/or Deadline

Your friends and/or peers will make you accountable. This will also provide excellent motivation, especially when they keep reminding you about your goal and the date that you said you were going to finish by.

One time, I told my friends I was going to lose thirty pounds in a month. My friends couldn't stop laughing. So I decided to offer a friendly wager. I was surprised when they offered 100-to-1 odds. At the end of thirty days, they were all waiting for me by my desk. They asked, "Did you go on a reverse diet?" They were right; I had actually gained weight. That's how I learned the power of telling others and your leader when you're going to start a task or project. Then you *have* to do it.

Give Yourself a Pep Talk

Difficult and unpleasant tasks can be tough, not only to start but also to finish. You must believe you can do it. Many times, we'll exaggerate how difficult or unpleasant a task will be before we even start. Try becoming your own cheerleader instead.

Eliminate, one by one, "reasons" why you can't start or get the task done. Talk yourself into just starting the task and trying to do it for 20–30 minutes. Focus on the reward. You may be surprised the next time you look up to see that you've been working for an hour!

Get More Information and/or Answers to Your Questions

Pick up the phone or get out of your chair and get the information or answers you need to overcome roadblocks. If it's important, don't wait. Often, the smallest piece of information or the smallest question answered will get us jumpstarted again. Don't use the excuse of not having enough information to put off tasks.

Create a Reward

Before you start that difficult or unpleasant task, think of a way to reward yourself when you complete it. It could be a new outfit, a meal at an expensive restaurant, a much-needed vacation, or just something you really like to do. Put that carrot in front of you so you see what's in it for you to complete that task.

People talk about improving the quality of their personal lives. Why not start by giving yourself mini-rewards that improve the quality of your personal life? Of course, you can always wait and hope until the end of the year!

Activity

Write down a task that you've been procrastinating starting on or completing. Write down what actions you can take to work through it.

You can also turn back to the Goal Form in Appendix C and use the nine steps to get started and complete your task or project that you've been putting off.

Appendix A

Timekeeping Journal

When I teach these lessons in person, I require my students to keep this Timekeeping Journal for one week prior to coming to class. If you are smart (which you obviously are, because you are studying these lessons!), you will do the same.

Keeping this journal, and analyzing its content, will allow you to determine for each task:

- Is this the best use of my time?
- Am I doing the right task at the right time?
- Are there any tasks that could be eliminated or put off?
- Could I cut down on the amount of time I'm spending on certain tasks?

The foundation for improving your time management skills is to know where your time is currently going. Through this analysis, you will find ways to improve how you're currently handling the tasks you're working on. Also, most people are so involved in day-to-day work that they never get a chance to step back and ask these questions.

You will use this throughout the lessons as a tool to help you set up a more productive day. By accepting the data in the Timekeeping Journal as representations of a typical day, you will look for ways to take advantage of your findings. You will begin to leave time for interruptions and the unexpected.

You will keep track of *tasks started* and *tasks completed.* This ratio can be a real problem. You will learn ways to be not only a good starter but also a great finisher.

I hear this all the time: "I have no personal life!" If you don't have one, then who has yours? This journal will show you why you feel this way, and you'll learn ways to achieve balance every day. (Don't worry—you'll still get all your work done.) You'll learn how to leave work on time.

Finally, this journal will help show you how to develop discipline. You will learn there is a time and place for everything and how to get into a "flow" every day, instead of jumping all over from task to task. You will then use that discipline to more effectively schedule your days.

KEEPING YOUR DAILY TIME RECORD

Begin by photocopying the blank Timekeeping Journal pages that follow. Make as many copies as the number of days during which you intend to keep track of your time. Ideally, you will fill out the journal for seven days, so you will need seven copies. Alternatively, you could keep track of your time for five days, for which you would need five photocopies. If, in the end, you only manage to journal your time for a few days, you will still receive enormous benefits; so please do the exercise.

To complete the Timekeeping Journal, you'll also need whatever system you use to keep track of your time, such as a day planner, Outlook software, a Palm Pilot handheld computer, or a pad of paper.

Here are the actual steps you will follow each day:

1. Put your worksheets on a clipboard and keep them handy with a pencil.
2. At the end of the day, before you're going to start keeping your daily time record, write your plan for tomorrow on the left side of the page.
3. Then the next morning when you come to work, start keeping track of your actual activities on the right side of the page.
4. Mentally commit your intentions to devote two minutes each half-hour to write down what has happened. (Repeat aloud: "I will find two minutes each half-hour to write on my worksheets.")
5. Don't let more than an hour pass without recording.
6. At the end of the day, review your record and correct or add anything that is needed. (Make sure that you can read what you have written.)

COMPLETING YOUR TIME MANAGEMENT IMPROVEMENT REPORT

At the end of the week, you will have all the necessary information you need to create your time management improvement report (located at the end of this journal). Review your daily time records and write down any patterns that you see. For example, "Between 8 and 9 every morning, I have more phone calls than I have in total for the rest of the morning. . . . Yet, this is the time I must complete the count report."

This type of notation represents an opportunity for more efficient time management of tasks, reduction of stress, and improvement of customer service. As you study the lessons in the book, be alert for solutions to your personal time management challenges.

Note the differences between what you planned and what really happened. This will make your future daily and weekly plans more realistic and achievable.

TIME MANAGEMENT IMPROVEMENT REPORT

Day# __________ Day of Week: __________ Date: __________

Activities begun/continued/ completed	**Interruptions/unexpected actions begun**
6:00 A.M.	6:00 A.M.
6:30	6:30
7:00	7:00
7:30	7:30
8:00	8:00
8:30	8:30
9:00	9:00
9:30	9:30
10:00	10:00
10:30	10:30
11:00	11:00
11:30	11:30
12:00 P.M. (Noon)	12:00 P.M. (Noon)
12:30	12:30
1:00	1:00
1:30	1:30

Day# ______________ *continued*

Activities begun/continued/ completed	**Interruptions/unexpected actions begun**
2:00	2:00
2:30	2:30
3:00	3:00
3:30	3:30
4:00	4:00
4:30	4:30
5:00	5:00
5:30	5:30
6:00	6:00
6:30	6:30
7:00	7:00
7:30	7:30
8:00	8:00
8:30	8:30
9:00	9:00
9:30	9:30
10:00	10:00

Day# ______________ *continued*

Activities begun/continued/ completed	Interruptions/unexpected actions begun
10:30	10:30
11:00	11:00
11:30	11:30
12:00 A.M. (Midnight)	12:00 A.M.

Day # ___ Completed;
Summary Day of Week: ________ Date: ________

Total activities begun: ______

Total activities completed: ______

Total interruptions: ______

Comments about This Day:

____

____

____

Summary Comments about This Week:

____

____

____

TIME MANAGEMENT IMPROVEMENT REPORT

Day# ____________ Day of Week: ____________ Date: ____________

Activities begun/continued/ completed	Interruptions/unexpected actions begun
6:00 A.M.	6:00 A.M.
6:30	6:30
7:00	7:00
7:30	7:30
8:00	8:00
8:30	8:30
9:00	9:00
9:30	9:30
10:00	10:00
10:30	10:30
11:00	11:00
11:30	11:30
12:00 P.M. (Noon)	12:00 P.M. (Noon)
12:30	12:30
1:00	1:00
1:30	1:30

Day# ____________ *continued*

Activities begun/continued/ completed	**Interruptions/unexpected actions begun**
2:00	2:00
2:30	2:30
3:00	3:00
3:30	3:30
4:00	4:00
4:30	4:30
5:00	5:00
5:30	5:30
6:00	6:00
6:30	6:30
7:00	7:00
7:30	7:30
8:00	8:00
8:30	8:30
9:00	9:00
9:30	9:30
10:00	10:00

Day# ______________ *continued*

Activities begun/continued/ completed	**Interruptions/unexpected actions begun**
10:30	10:30
11:00	11:00
11:30	11:30
12:00 A.M. (Midnight)	12:00 A.M.

Day # ___ Completed;
Summary Day of Week: _________ Date: _________

Total activities begun: _______

Total activities completed: _______

Total interruptions: _______

Comments about This Day:

____

____

____

Summary Comments about This Week:

____

____

____

TIME MANAGEMENT IMPROVEMENT REPORT

Day# ____________ Day of Week: ____________ Date: ____________

Activities begun/continued/ completed	Interruptions/unexpected actions begun
6:00 A.M.	6:00 A.M.
6:30	6:30
7:00	7:00
7:30	7:30
8:00	8:00
8:30	8:30
9:00	9:00
9:30	9:30
10:00	10:00
10:30	10:30
11:00	11:00
11:30	11:30
12:00 P.M. (Noon)	12:00 P.M. (Noon)
12:30	12:30
1:00	1:00
1:30	1:30

Day# ______________ *continued*

Activities begun/continued/ completed	**Interruptions/unexpected actions begun**
2:00	2:00
2:30	2:30
3:00	3:00
3:30	3:30
4:00	4:00
4:30	4:30
5:00	5:00
5:30	5:30
6:00	6:00
6:30	6:30
7:00	7:00
7:30	7:30
8:00	8:00
8:30	8:30
9:00	9:00
9:30	9:30
10:00	10:00

Day# ______ *continued*

Activities begun/continued/ completed	**Interruptions/unexpected actions begun**
10:30	10:30
11:00	11:00
11:30	11:30
12:00 A.M. (Midnight)	12:00 A.M.

Day # ___ Completed;
Summary Day of Week: ______ Date: ______

Total activities begun: ______

Total activities completed: ______

Total interruptions: ______

Comments about This Day:

______

______

______

Summary Comments about This Week:

______

______

______

APPENDIX B

Time Management Action Plan

Name three time management strategies, discussed in the book, that you're going to implement as soon as you go back to work.

1. ____

____

____

2. ____

____

____

3. ____

____

____

Name one strategy in each of the following areas that you're going to implement within the next seven days:

1. Goal setting ______________________________
2. Organizing ______________________________
3. Managing priorities ______________________________
4. Finding more time ______________________________
5. Controlling your desk ______________________________
6. Handling interruptions ______________________________
7. Managing and writing e-mail ______________________________
8. Delegating ______________________________
9. Planning meetings ______________________________
10. Managing procrastination ______________________________

APPENDIX C

Goal Form

This form can be utilized two different ways. One, for a project or task you're currently putting off, and two, for goal setting at the end of the year for next year. If you are using the form for a project or task skip the first line, "Organizational goal." Just write your desired end result in "Your goal." Then follow all of the steps identified at the end of Chapter 2. If you are using the form for goal setting, ask your boss for one of his or her goals and write it in the top line in "Organizational goal." Then write your goal that will support your boss's goal in "Your goal." Make sure the goal follows all of the steps described in the Chapter 2.

TEAM PERFORMANCE PLANNER

Organizational goal:

Your goal:

Specific Activities Needed to Complete Your Goal	Who Is Needed?	Work on It When?	Signoff	Deadline

Index

F

G

N

O

P

Q

R

S

T

V

W

Notes

Notes

About the Author

Kenneth Zeigler is a top expert on time management, organization, and productivity improvement. He has authored many articles on these subjects, and he was the first author to discover the problem is not the system people use, but rather their organization skill set.

Ken has served in senior management at firms such as Pillsbury, Hughes, Quaker Oats, Merrill Lynch, and Dean Witter. As a consultant he has advised clients such as Hertz, Toys "R" Us, the Federal Reserve, the Comptroller of the Currency, and Fidelity.

Ken attended the University of Minnesota as an undergraduate, where he was a member of the varsity football team, and then completed graduate work in advertising and finance at the University of Illinois. He lives in Nashville with his wife Mary Beth and his sons, Zachary and Nicholas.

Visit his web site at *http://www.kztraining.com.*

About the Author